CHARACTER, COMPETENCE, AND COMMITMENT...THE MEASURE OF A LEADER

Leadership philosophies, principles and observations of a career Air Force Combat Controller

by

Paul "Vinnie" Venturella

authorHOUSE®

AuthorHouse™
1663 Liberty Drive, Suite 200
Bloomington, IN 47403
www.authorhouse.com
Phone: 1-800-839-8640

First published by AuthorHouse 8/6/2007

ISBN: 978-1-4343-2170-1 (sc)

Library of Congress Control Number: 2007905130

Printed in the United States of America
Bloomington, Indiana

This book is printed on acid-free paper.

Dedicated to the men who have mentored me and to those I have mentored.

Also dedicated to Tammie.

She's my wife; she's a saint; and has supported me every step of the way.

CONTENTS

Introduction

(May 2007; Second Edition)

I finished my first edition of this book in September 2003. I had it made into a book (not published) to give to a group of personal friends and my family. I received tremendous feedback from the first edition so I decided to write a second edition and have it published.

This edition is more meant for "prime time." The first one was a little crude, blunt, and probably <u>too</u> straightforward for the average reader. So I updated my original edition; adjusted some of the lessons; and added a few other thoughts along the way since September 2003.

Throughout my career in the Air Force I was a leader that led. I tried to become a student of leadership in order to make my own style better. I truly tried to make myself, my troops and my unit better.

As you read over these pages of insight and lessons learned, please understand this is what I've found worked for me or others I thought were successful. Some people I've come across haven't done these and still had some level of success. You can punch holes in every philosophy, not just mine. That's not the intent of this book, but rather to share some of what I've learned.

I consider myself a leader and teacher. I've spent and will spend my life mentoring those around me.

This is what I've found works for the "majority" of people. As the "Boss" said in *Cool Hand Luke*, "Some men, you just can't reach." To some it doesn't matter what you do, they just don't get it. Newman still did it his way. Don't fret, stay focused and on course and trust me you'll be successful. Don't let the 10% get you down. Take care of your lead dogs and they'll take care of you.

I learned a lot from watching others. In essence I saw what worked and more importantly, what didn't. I capitalized on my own mistakes and those of others. No lesson is learned better than the hard way.

I've read a lot of books on leadership in my life. Being a leader was what I desired to be good at aside from my job. The only way to get better is first of all experience it, but also you must receive training and education.

I took the responsibility of leadership with fervor. I would assess every situation and if I needed to lead, I would. If I didn't (for example some times you must let those below you run with the ball) it was because I didn't feel a need or it wasn't my place.

I've heard that the Air Force doesn't actually teach "leadership." I don't know if you can <u>teach</u> leadership per se. I don't really have an opinion on whether the AF taught it or not. What I believe is the AF put us in an environment, and the leaders led. Sure, the AF presented some education and training, but how do you learn how to lead, except to lead? I believe they taught knowledge, skills and abilities, but the actual act of leading was nurtured and developed over time.

You're a product of your environment: if people are put in a place that requires leadership, the leaders will lead. They learn by doing and the sled dogs (see chapter on *Sled Dogs*) learn by watching and then doing when it's their turn. Leadership is a responsibility and an art, not a job or duty title.

I used to worry about trying to make everyone happy. It's impossible. So eventually I realized if I could look in the mirror and knew I was doing the right things that should be fine. Or if my boss told me I was doing the right things that also gave me validation. I believe if you "do the right thing" then people will ultimately be happy. How can they not be?

When your commander has to make those hard decisions and they all do, ensure he hears validation from those below him. If he's right, tell him he's right, especially if it's an issue pertaining to a hard personnel issue or one regarding a moral dilemma.

Leaders lead. If you have to be told to lead, you aren't the leader. If someone has to ask, who's in charge...they aren't. Leaders are responsible for leading and taking care of their organizations. They are the ones that take a task or a group of dudes, and say, "follow me."

Leaders aren't afraid to make mistakes; they look at it as an opportunity to grow. What better way to learn than learning from a mistake. However, if you keep making the same mistakes you need to do a self-assessment and/or your boss needs to kick you in the backside.

If no one says anything about you (good or bad) you aren't doing enough or not doing anything. Leaders are out front. When it's good or bad leaders lead. Leaders are heard, seen and hopefully emulated.

This book has some areas of plain or blunt language. It's designed to make a point or that's how I really say things. I gave appropriate credit where it was due. I used a fair amount of direct quotes, movie quotes and paraphrases. This book is meant to teach and even though it was written when I was in the Air Force and the focus is military or small-unit leadership; it is applicable regardless of environment. I write from the male perspective. Don't lose the lesson because I didn't say "he/she."

I hope you learn some lessons from my experiences. When you are in your own world, whatever or wherever that may be, exercise some leadership. Lead your people and they will make the mission happen.

My Three "C's"

Character / Competence / Commitment

I am and I promise character, competence, and commitment. At the risk of oversimplifying what I believe are the most important attributes in a person, my three C's encapsulate the total package. They are just words, but words that mean more to me than most. I am a huge believer in and preacher of the Air Force Core Values (Integrity, Service and Excellence). I believed if you truly adhered to or lived by the core values nothing else could be asked of you, because you're already where you need to be. Same thing with my three "C's." Incidentally, I was doing the AF Core Values even before the Air Force developed them. Integrity; Service; and Excellence were the order of the day in *La casa de Vinman* before I joined the Air Force.

Character:

To me this is the most important. Character is huge. Integrity, loyalty, guts, maturity…these are all part of character. When you are in deep suck and you act like you've been there before…it's no big deal. Lombardi said the same thing with reference to the end zone; if you ever get there, act like you've been there before. That's character. Doing what is right when no one is looking. That's character. Doing those little things. Remaining loyal above and below you. Being honest. Telling it like it is. Doing the right thing all the time. Not whining about stuff to those that you outrank. Not talking smack about the head shed or unit itself. Not airing your unit's dirty laundry in public. That's character. It's a key part of the foundation of a man.

Character is when someone can count on you, no matter what. Character is when you aren't at work and your boss doesn't think you're screwing off. Character is when you are expected to do something, aren't told to do it, and you still do it. Character is sucking up a bad deal because you're supposed to.

Character is when your commander can count on you every day especially game day. No matter what, I would be there right there next to him. He didn't have to wonder if I'm hurt, sick, taking it easy, finding an excuse to get out of work, whatever. He knew, because I had character, that I was his rock; I was the unit's rock. The one that anyone and everyone could count on. He knew on "game day;" I'd be there. It didn't matter if some had legitimate excuses why they couldn't perform on "game day" those with character did and do, no matter what, because it was "game day."

With reference to character, Secretary of Defense Donald Rumsfeld said the below quote with reference to the events following 9/11:

I close with a thought that occurred to me as President Bush spoke on Saturday…about the qualities that make America special and exceptional. He talked about civility, courage, character—reminders that the strength that matters most is not the strength of arms, but the strength of character; character expressed in service to something larger than ourselves. And if that is an ultimate safeguard, then we are indeed a blessed nation.

Character is not made during adversity, it's revealed.

Competence:

You've got to be good at your job. The Air Force pays us to be an expert at our job based on our current rank. As a Combat Controller (or any job) you've got to be an expert at your job at that particular level in your career. I know more than you about being a Senior (there are 9 enlisted ranks…a Senior or SMSgt is an E-8), but as a TSgt (E-6) there are certain things you should be the master of. For example, you need to know your radios inside and out, how to conduct Terminal Attack Control, and how to jump; that's what you call technical competence.

The Air Force still expects you to do more. For example, write EPRs (annual appraisal reports called Enlisted Performance Reports), provide feedback, manage resources, etc. That's what I'll call organizational competence. Stuff you have to do because you're in the Air Force. You need both types of competence. I used to laugh at those guys that just wanted to worry about their rucksack and nothing more. Trust me, it showed they didn't worry about nothing more than their rucksack. As you progress up in rank, more is expected out of you. You must take on more responsibility.

Do you think your troop's EPR got written by itself? Do you think your team gets funds all by themselves? How do you think your team got its new gear? Bottom line: you need both types of competence. I understand that Spec Ops (Special Operations is a broad category of men, mission, and machine denoting a higher and more sensitive level of activities) the best operators should only worry about training and keeping the knife sharp until it's time to do the mission and can argue for it. But there are a whole slew of issues that require attention simply because we're in the military.

Don't spend valuable time and energy whining about something that will never get changed.

You must take a share of the responsibility to become competent at your job. The Air Force (AF) or any organization for that matter, trains you to a certain level. To get to the next level requires personal involvement. I used to appreciate it when I'd see sled dogs studying a new procedure or taking it upon themselves to learn and perfect a new piece of gear. If you aren't one of those guys you aren't doing your job.

Leaders are responsible for getting their folks trained. A unit that doesn't make training a high priority is screwed. Not to get deep but the military is an extension of national power. It is called upon to exert its will on the enemy. That will, requires training, so when we're called upon we can execute.

Commitment:

Did you ever pay attention to the Oath of Enlistment; or did you just rush to get it done so you can run to finance and get your bonus? That was back when they actually issued checks. "I do solemnly swear..." What about the Code of Conduct? "I'm prepared to give my life..." What we do in the military is important. We've volunteered, and volunteered more than once. We have a higher calling, we've volunteered to do what it takes to defend our constitution and great nation and do what it takes to defend our freedoms, to give our life for our country if it came to that. Patton said we shouldn't die for our country but make the enemy give his life for his country, and he's right. But that's the ultimate commitment, one that's for your country.

Why did/do I do what I did/do? I don't know, I guess I thought that's what I was supposed to do. A theory of mine is this: on the day you retire people will say how awesome you are and give you a nice shadow box and talk really nice and all and some will even remember you when you're gone but, it really doesn't mean anything. The only people it matters to are your family and the guy you look at when you're shaving in the morning at 0400. When I look in the mirror, I know for a fact I led from the front, exceeded the standards, was 100% committed, 100% of the time. Well, me and the Man upstairs any way.

Commitment is more than just the paragraph above. You knew a man's commitment when the chips were down or it was tough. You really knew when you were staring at a 3-6 month deployment. Sure it's easy to appear committed when you sleep next to Momma every night. You just have to fake it for those 8 hours I see you. But when Uncle Sam really needs you and you perform without so much as a peep, that's commitment. It means doing whatever it takes, whenever, wherever.

Watch people's reaction when someone tells them something that at that instant they perceive is bad or a raw deal. Their body language gives it away. It gives away their lack of commitment. Commitment is when you roger up and press on.

Commitment is service to your fellow comrades, unit, AF and country. Commitment is being a professional everyone can count on, not matter what or no matter when.

EXPECT HIGH STANDARDS AND YOU'LL GET HIGH STANDARDS...DON'T AND YOU WON'T.

Go into any unit, business or home and do a quick assessment. If it appears neat and orderly; looks squared away; the people look happy and motivated; a lot can be said of the leader, manager, or family. As a supervisor, leader, or manager if you don't care what your troops are doing, they probably won't either. If you don't expect them to get their hair cut or shine their boots, they won't. However, if you expect your men to look squared away, they will. If you expect them to do the best they can possibly do, and not just meet the standard, they will.

Now of course standards are a matter of perspective. What I think is meeting the standard, some may think as exceeding the standard. So where do you draw the line? That's a pretty good question. My theory was if I was your boss and/or out ranked you, my perspective is the one we use. That's why I got paid more than you.

A caution that I learned the hard way...my standards are/were so high for myself that I often (and mistakenly) expected those same standards of my troops. My troops' standards could still be below mine and still be exceeding "the" standard. For me to expect what I do, from my troops in a lot of cases would have been unfair. I do what I do, because of who I am. I don't know if it was right or wrong, that's just the way it was.

I've been around excellence my whole life. And one common denominator (there are more) was the people especially the leaders of the organizations, demanded excellence. They expected high standards. They made excellence the standard.

The lesson here is your people need to know what is expected of them. If the expectations are high, their performance will more often than not be high and subsequently exceed the standards. Demand your people measure up.

The 10% Rule

Regardless how perfect your unit is or how good your leadership style is or whatever, I've found some men just don't get it. Some just don't conform. I call it the *10% rule*. Sometimes it's a lot less than that, but the principle still applies…you'll have those that just don't respond. They aren't worthless (well not all of them), so you have to find "something" that works. Now if you let him do what he wants (not recommended), ride his back (takes a lot of energy), or whatever, you still need to at least get some level out of him.

The 10% rule means know from the start you won't make everyone happy all the time and some men just won't respond positively to you. The problem is when leadership treats "the 10%" the same as your lead dogs at awards, decorations or EPR time. Enlisted Performance Reports were annual appraisals using a 1 to 5 scale. I didn't and won't treat the 10% the same as my lead dogs. You have a choice, get on my page or suffer the consequences. The consequences didn't include a 5 on your EPR or NCO of the Quarter. Don't fret, press on with your program and take care of your sled dogs.

Leaders have a responsibility for all of their people. You can't just throw them away. You can fire them and have them work for a lower ranking guy, but you can't throw them away in most situations. However, there were times when I wished to get rid of those that consistently didn't measure up and never tried to; but was successful on a few occasions of getting rid of some dead wood. Maybe if you buried a few of them alive in a cornfield after pummeling them with baseball bats, the rest would get in line. The point of the 10% rule is understand they're out there; use all your tools in your toolbox to get them to a level you need them.

Time Management

There are as many "time management" schemes and philosophies out there as there are people it seems. Most had their own system. Some didn't have any system. My system was simple: Get my work done; prioritize when I had to; and delegate as much as possible. Duty hours to me were a guide. I didn't stop working because it was 1600 (4:00 PM) or not start work until 0700 (7:00 AM) if I had work to do.

As I got older and had more responsibility I had to prioritize my day more than when I was a sled dog. I would come to work first almost every day I can remember...more on that later. When no one was at work (not during duty hours) I would study or read (there is always something you could be studying or reading) for about an hour to hour and a half then I could work for about an hour to hour and a half before everyone showed up. Then I'd do my PT (physical training is simply working out) and the rest of my day I had planned out.

A lot of time is wasted socially...BSing in the office or hanging out in the team room telling war stories. Some of it was waste, but some of it was valid. It was those times where you built relationships, and those

12

matter. But a key thing in time management is to cut out the waste.

I was so concerned with ensuring everything I did was first rate or as near perfect that I could make it. Some would say that's a losing battle. Well those are the naysayers who look for an excuse why they couldn't measure up. Because I strived for perfection, I knew I had to work late or come in during my off time to get my work done. A main reason was I would attempt to never miss any suspense, regardless of what was going on. Another reason was I knew if I didn't get "XYZ" done, it would be there tomorrow, along with whatever tomorrow brought.

Some would say working overtime is not good time management. I would say, if I didn't work overtime my work didn't get done or didn't get done at the quality I wanted. All I know is my work spoke for itself. It's easy to question someone and call them a workaholic negatively, but who else was going to get a unit through an ORI (a major inspection) when our procedures were absolutely crap a year prior? Or who was going to get a unit ready to deploy for war and succeed in war? You don't succeed in battle or when the pressure is on only working 8 hours a day.

My point of the preceding two paragraphs is to point out regardless of how much you delegate, or how efficient your processes become, leaders still need to take care of those things that, regardless of the time of day or time of year, have to get taken care of. When I was younger I knew there was nothing I couldn't do. As I got older and had more responsibility I realized that I couldn't do <u>everything</u>. You can put only a certain amount of ping pong balls on a plate. As you put more than can fit some start to fall off. So what do you do? Prioritize.

Another thing is to use some form of medium to manage time. Mine was a Day Runner. I bought one in 1990; before they were cool and everyone had one, and have been using one ever since. (I use Microsoft Outlook® now and "live" by the Calendar.) Some people use a PDA. Whatever you use, you need something. It could be something as simple as a notebook. I would put every appointment in my calendar and around those "hard" times I would plan my work. My work was wide and varied whether it was operating, paper work, thinking stuff up, working projects, associating with people, it didn't matter.

Part of my Day Runner included a stenographer notebook that was kept with it at all times. On that notebook I had my "to do list." I had "gotta dos" everyday. I had to keep the endless correspondence moving; I had to associate with most of the head shed; I had to ensure my troops were on track; etc. And this doesn't even take into account the major projects I always had my hands in that were long term but had milestones that had to be met. Your "to do list" doesn't take into account those "short notice" suspenses, that all of us had to do. But as soon as you get a short notice task it should go on your to do list.

Emails are simple. Email is not a job it's a communication device. Get on…say what you need to say…and get off. Remember, however, that email may be misunderstood by the receiver based on many reasons. So I did my best to make them as simple and clear as possible, within reason. Select a time or times during your day to conduct email correspondence. If you allow email to run your day; you will waste a severe amount of time. I have never and hopefully will never have a reason to get a "CrackBerry." Whatever happened to the phone? Use email to communicate as efficiently as possible; but don't let it rule your day.

I don't deny the CrackBerry is a valuable tool. But some people have taken this to a new ridiculous level. Here is when you know you are a goof. When you are sending emails on your CrackBerry to a dude who is in the same meeting as you. Are you kidding me? Use email efficiently and effectively and don't be a goof.

I spent a lot of my day dealing with people, whether in person, on the phone or via email. This took a lot of time. Every single person that wanted some time, I would give what I could when I could. If I didn't have time when they asked I would ask them to come back or make an appointment. My time was important, but more importantly was I wanted to give the person every bit of my attention. They came to me because their issue was important, so I owed them my time.

So plan your day. Use an organization medium. Don't revisit minor issues. Save time where able. Prioritize your work. Get your work done. And delegate where able. We're paid to make things happen not count batteries. (A great BS detail at my first duty station...we literally had to count batteries and there were hundreds of them.) That's what sled dogs do; you must keep the sled dogs doing what they're supposed to be doing not doing the sled dogs' jobs.

IF YOU DON'T MAINTAIN A STANDARD, YOU'VE JUST ESTABLISHED A NEW ONE.

One of the best Chiefs (E-9--the ranking enlisted man) I was ever lucky enough to have served with was CMSgt Mike Lampe. He was what you'd expect in a Spec Ops man. He ruled the roost at a unit we were assigned to at the time. Sure the commander was in charge…on paper, but Chief Lampe ran the show. He was so revered by those in our community that three Warfighters (Generals that are personally tasked by the President to execute wars) in a row, asked him to stay on as his Senior Enlisted Advisor. For those that know what that means, realize, there is no higher amount of respect a Combatant Commander can give you.

Chief Lampe said this to us. For example, if a guy comes late to work and you don't square it away, you've just said, it's okay to come late to work. Sure people make mistakes and deserve chances, especially your lead dogs. But if you don't maintain a standard, you've just established a new one.

One of the things I found a lot of and it bothered me, was unwillingness to correct substandard behavior. It was like people didn't care, or were oblivious, or didn't want confrontation, I don't know. Bottom line it's your duty to correct substandard behavior.

If you are afraid of confrontation and go through a whole career not squaring things away that you should have, then imagine how good your troops and unit would be if you exerted your duty. It's not that I would nit-pick, although I've been accused of that, but I wouldn't let a lot of crap slide that was wrong.

When I was a sled dog, I used to say, "If I'm ever in charge, that stuff ain't going to happen." There were times when the head shed would not make certain guys show up to work on time or make them do their PT or let them slide on basic standards. What was worse was when things deserved the hammer or even UCMJ action (the legal rules of the military), and nothing was done; it said to everyone else, standards aren't maintained. And you could see the Chief's point relived daily.

Maintain your organization's standards.

WORRY ABOUT THE SMALL STUFF AND THE BIG STUFF WILL TAKE CARE OF ITSELF.

Don't take this one out of context. I don't mean worry about trivial or inconsequential things and forget about why we're really here. On the contrary, it's not trivial; it is attention to detail. After all, the big stuff is nothing but a bunch of small stuff put together. Think about the huge successes America, the military, the Air Force or a particular unit has had. Sure those are big picture, but it wouldn't have happened without taking care of the details. To have kicked the living crap out of Saddam's regime and the Taliban took details. Men on the ground had the proper COMSEC (Communications Security--that magic that makes your radio secure from those that don't have the same COMSEC as you), the proper map, the right heading and distance, the right grid coordinate. They had to get to that location, locate their target, talk on that hugely expensive radio and put that hot steel on target. All small by themselves, but the end result was victory in war.

Attention to detail means doing those little things. Coming to work on time, doing your PT, shining your boots, adhering to customs and courtesies. If you don't worry about the little things in peacetime, why should I expect you would worry about them in wartime? Keeping the little things squared away is a sign of good character.

I think some men thought that since they were Spec Ops that they could run a "fly by night" operation simply because they were Spec Ops. This isn't the case. If anything, our responsibilities mandated a more concerted effort on details, since we had so few people and they were often on their own making things happen.

A key thing to remember when trying to teach your people attention to detail is to not hammer someone for one or a few infractions over a period of time. However, if lack of attention to detail occurs often over a period of time, then you need to correct it. Sure it's easy to explain each of 15 instances of lack of attention to detail away. By itself, one is not a big deal. But 15 are a trend and demand corrective action.

The best troops, teams and units were those that took care of the details.

Initiative

This is what separates great NCOs from good NCOs.

Noncommissioned officers are those mid-level enlisted ranks that hack the mission. Senior NCOs (SNCO) are those upper-level enlisted ranks that make things happen and keep it all together.

I've come across some phenomenal people in my career. Most were really good at their jobs. But those that were the best, all the time, were those that selflessly showed initiative. Doing what needed to be done without being told. I expect things to get done by sled dogs. Some sled dogs expect you to tell them what to do. If you aren't telling them what to do, some think there isn't anything to do. Initiative means doing those things you know need to be done, without being told.

Here's a simple test. If the boss cuts everyone out of the shop early for the day, watch who bolts that second. Watch who stays and nugs through the work he was working on, or uses it as a time to get something done. Sure, it's nice to cut the sled dogs out early if they've earned it, but if the same people bolt every time or say there isn't anything to do they may lack initiative.

One of my favorite excuses why people didn't do XYZ without being told was "that's not my job." Wrongo… wrongo! Because you are in uniform and some job or BS detail needed taken care of, you were responsible for its completion.

Initiative also means when given a seemingly impossible requirement, you make it happen. Let's say I asked you to do a task important to the unit or to me or even the commander. A man with initiative, regardless what else he had to do, would relish the opportunity. A man with initiative would do everything in his power to get it done.

Look for initiative in your units. It will appear; saddle up those horses and let them run. They're the ones that are making you a great unit.

SLED DOGS

People have heard me use the term "sled dogs" for quite some time. To some it's derogatory. To those that know, it's a term of endearment. If you know anything about sled dogs (the ones that pull the sleds like in the Iditarod—the sled dog race in Alaska), you'll understand the concept. Visualize a sled dog team. There's normally one up front. How do you think he got there? He's the lead dog for a reason. Now take a team for instance. That front dog is your "lead" dog; your #1 go to guy. He's the guy that leads the rest of the team. Who's the guy on the sled? He could be any level of leadership: the NCOIC, the flight commander, the unit commander…whoever. The size of the guy on the sled is relative to the team.

The concept is best when compared to a regular Special Tactics team. Special Tactics is a capability. It consists of a bunch of specialists in different jobs that provide warfighters that Airmanship they so desperately need. Like a sled dog team, some times they need to be whipped, yelled at, hugged or loved on. They are yours and they depend on you. If you always whip them then as soon as you untie them they're out of there, if they don't chew your butt up first. If you love on them too much, they'll get soft and lazy. They need to know that the guy on the sled is still the Alpha Male (see chapter on *The Alpha Male*). Just imagine when you see a smooth team. Same thing with your "sled dogs." What a force: 18 dudes moving all in the same direction…to one goal. It's beautiful.

Sled dogs are who do the preponderance of the work. Sure they may be senior sled dogs but the concept remains: they're your mission hackers. They are the ones doing the mission. They're the ones doing the scut (the dirty jobs that have to get done) work. Take care of them.

So when I say sled dogs, it's because I love them. I've been a regular dog, a lead dog and the musher. It's a matter of perspective or where you are in your career, as to your location on the sled.

LEAD BY EXAMPLE...FROM THE FRONT

"What should I be doing?" "What is the right thing to do?" All you have to do is watch me. I tried my best to lead from the front. I was at work early, did my PT, busted my hump to do the best I could every day, and took what I did seriously. Everything I did I tried to do the best, fastest and most effective. It probably isn't healthy to treat life like a competition, but I did. I don't know why, I just thought that's what I was supposed to do. Bottom line: I practiced what I preached.

I wouldn't and didn't ask anyone to do anything that I hadn't already done or wouldn't do. When people saw me at work first, doing PT every day, and doing those little things, I can only assume it had a positive effect. I know it did on me when I was a sled dog and saw an older guy doing all those things.

Leadership by example assumes you are doing the right things. But leadership by example could be doing the wrong things. Look at a team or unit where the guy in charge is all screwed up. When they don't present a positive example. When they don't care about standards or discipline. Lead by example...positively.

Not everyone could keep up with me and some didn't care to. That's fine. My standards are/were higher than most. That's not the point. The point is being a good example for your troops and unit. Let the world know you can be counted on…every day.

Leadership by example simply means doing what you're supposed to be doing. It's easy to say "do this, do that." It's a lot harder to actually act. Action speaks louder than words. For example, and this actually happened: a team leader took his team out for a run around the base. Well they ran, he rode his bike. Who cares why, except he wasn't leading by example. What do you think the sled dogs thought? It wasn't positive. Sled dogs need to see you right next to them doing what they're doing. And if you're really squared away, you should be doing it better than them.

Now a 20-year-old stud needs to be smoking me in PT. If you aren't then check yourself. So it doesn't mean much when you talk junk about it, you're supposed to be running faster than me.

When the boss needs a volunteer for some project, leadership by example means you volunteer. Not because he expects you to, even though he does, but because it's the right thing to do. Be an example…be "the" example.

Vision

A vision is an overarching theme that should provide a road to achievement. It is normally "bigger picture" but may detail the heart of an organization's business or point to a part of it. An organization without a vision is normally stuck in the day-to-day grind; the status quo; and may never truly become successful. The same can be said about an individual without a vision.

A vision should help you attain your goals and objectives. It should be challenging, insightful and cause action.

A vision about the enlisted force I've carried with me for some time is as follows:

Unit of highly motivated, energetic, professional and disciplined Airmen who exceed the standards for character, competence and commitment.

A vision should not be impossible to attain but shouldn't be so basic as to not energize an organization or a group of individuals. A vision must have buy-in from the members of an organization in order to be realized. Sure a lot of people can develop nice "eye charts" and displays or whatever talking about all the things an organization does, can do, or wants to do.

During these fast-paced times in our military it is often times difficult if not impossible to think about the future. Sometimes we can barely keep up with the here and now. But if you always practice crisis management you'll never get any better and all you'll do is deal with the "one meter targets" so to speak. A vision takes a look at the 500-meter targets. However, there is a lot to be said about men and units that are masters of crisis management. When the chips are down it's these men that are making things happen.

We used the analogy of the priority of targets to compare to every day issues: the closer it is the more timely the attention it may get. The farther it is away may allow you to not worry about it at that instant, but it was still there and eventually needed to get taken care of.

A bought into vision will give a unit a long-term look at themselves. With that look, lower levels of the organization can do their own part to attain it.

You can tell when a unit doesn't have a vision. They can't ever seem to get out from under "today's" issues. They have a bunch of personnel that don't have job satisfaction and/or treat the job as a "9 to 5" gig. They don't accomplish anything big, but may have small successes. They usually don't have a very good recognition program. Don't forget about the 10% rule. Even a unit with a great vision, that's bought in to still has those that don't care about anything except collecting a check.

A unit with a vision is going somewhere. They have long-term plans. They set goals and then go out and accomplish them. They normally have a highly motivated force. They have people that truly want to be in an organization.

Sure, having a vision isn't all there is to a successful unit, there are tons of things a unit must have. But if you don't know where you're going how will you get there?

Ensure your unit implements a vision to give it a direction, a long-term view of itself, a uniting theme. As a leader ensure your vision enhances the unit's. Inspire people to attain far-reaching goals. Challenge them to bust through the status quo and "business as usual."

An organization or individual with a vision captures imagination, a can-do attitude, and a desire for achievement.

MAKE IT HAPPEN

Did you ever hear, "I can't stand 'yes' men"? Here's my spin on it. I want "yes" men. "Yes, I'll do that." "Yes, I'll square that away." "Yes, I'll make it happen." Don't tell me why you can't or won't. Don't tell me no, without even exploring the potential of making something happen. Get off your butt and get it done. Just do it. Tell me what you're going to do to make it happen and do it. Don't let obstacles get in your way; go over, around, under or through. Just get it done.

Make it happen doesn't mean break the law... well not on a normal day. I've cut corners and made stuff happen because I had to and it was the right thing to do. I didn't kill anyone who didn't deserve it or steal something that I/the unit didn't need. Seriously, it says a lot about a person who can, when faced with a challenge, gets the job done. *"Anyone can do it if it's easy; it's the hard that makes it great."* (Tom Hanks, *A League of their Own*)

The guys I took care of time and time again made it happen. They didn't let obstacles get in their way. You knew when you presented them with a task all you had to do was stand back and they'd take care of it.

Spec Ops must not be allowed to fit into a "cookie cutter" paradigm. We must be allowed to push the limits, whatever that may be. In Spec Ops you are paid to make things happen. There aren't books or checklists on the battlefield telling you what to do every step of the way. There are only you, your men, and your ingenuity, experience, and brain.

I can't count how many times I would hear excuses why something wasn't done. Even really well-veiled excuses with apparently legitimate reasons why Airman Shmucketelly didn't do XYZ. Bottom line; make it happen, just get it done.

Exceeding the Standard is the Standard

People talk about standards all the time. I do also. To me standards are specific and known. Those who throw it around in general terms probably don't exceed the standards. It's their way of telling their troops to get their crap together, but they need to look in the mirror. My theory is if all you do is meet Air Force standards, you're a 3 maybe a 2. To earn that 5, whether in the Air Force or in life, you've got to exceed the standards. Give a little extra. Get up earlier than the competition. Shine your boots a little better than the guy whose spit shin is good but not as good as mine. Run faster than you did yesterday. Do your job the better than you have to.

I used to hate the term "close enough for government work." I don't know where it came from, but it was well before my time. But it's still used to this day. It means the government really doesn't care about the standards of a particular job or issue…WRONG!

I was specific on what I expected my troops to do and be. I would lay out in detail what it took to earn a firewall 5 on their EPR. A "firewall" meant that on the front of an EPR the markings for a bunch of criteria were rated all the way to the right meaning the best. It was expected they would at least meet the standards. To some, meeting the standards was a 5. Those hard headed enough to test me found out after one reporting period how serious I was about standards. I didn't care that the rest of the career field or even the Air Force pencil whipped good EPRs; that's their problem.

If you don't exceed the standards you won't be truly successful. The "standard" just gets you in the door, exceeding the standard gets you to the finish line...first. Everyone likes a winner.

STRIVE FOR PERFECTION

Perfection is often an allusive goal. But who strives for "mediocrity?" Mediocre people, that's who. If you strive for perfection, everything you do will be exceeding the standard. My wife used to say 'You're never satisfied.' Once you've reached a level of satisfaction, I believe you start to get soft. Ask any pro team who won their sports' championship the year before. It's hard to stay on top, to reach the next level.

I strived for it in almost everything. There is always a better, faster, less expensive or more efficient way to do something. Find it. Incorporate it.

Some people would say, "I'm not perfect" about themselves. I know that; no one is. But to use it as your excuse why you don't meet or exceed standards is just that, an excuse. Striving for perfection brings out the best in people. The human is an amazing creature. It has boundless limits if you train to attain them. If you try for perfection you'll be better than if you didn't, plain and simple.

If you look at an EPR it has 5 ratings on it. Five means exceeding the standard. It appeared that a 5 was given out too often in my opinion. If you came to work, did what was asked, met the standard in most things…but did nothing more, technically that's a 3. But if you strive for perfection and exceeding the standard then that's a 5.

Sure, I could still meet my boss's expectations of a "5" and have more personal time and not worry about the little things, and all that if I didn't strive for perfection so much. But that's not how I am. Do you think anyone talks junk about Bill Parcells', Bill Belichick's, or Bill Cowher's ways of coaching a football team? No, they revere them. And these guys wrote the book on perfection and exceeding the standards. Sure it's great when you win, but whether these guys win or lose that season they strive for perfection. So should you.

COMMUNITY SERVICE

In the military we have numerous opportunities to give to the community we serve. When I say "community" I mean your unit, base, AF or local community. As a member of the military, especially a SNCO, you should give to the community to make it better.

Some would say community service is for those that are trying to suck up or for those SNCOs that are trying to make eight or nine (the two highest enlisted ranks.) Wrong answer. Community service is the right thing to do. When I was a sled dog I was serving my community.

A while back, I heard the American Red Cross was collecting "care packages" for American servicemen in Bagram, Afghanistan. I took the project and ran with it. The reason wasn't because I was trying to kiss butt or make rank. I've been on the other end of those care packages from some unnamed person in a conflict and remembered how good it made me feel. So I solicited for donations, gathered our unit donation and presented it to the local ARC chapter.

Apparently, the ARC sent the package and then the station chief sent me a nice letter thanking the unit and me. It made me feel good and I know that the unit donation made those in that place feel just a little better, all things considered.

As a member of the profession of arms you have a responsibility to serve the community. It's understood our #1 responsibility when it comes to serving is the simple fact of actually being in the military. What I mean is above and beyond service.

Collect donations for some local organization that are helping those in need. Volunteer to run a project on the base that supports a Morale Welfare and Recreation issue or a professional development issue. Run a project at your unit that enhances morale. These things just don't happen, someone is squaring them away. Do you think the Top III Induction Ceremony (ceremony honoring those entering the SNCO ranks known as the Top III) happens by itself? No it doesn't. It takes volunteers to make it happen.

What if a troop just doesn't want to support the community? You need to try and motivate him and show him the benefits of supporting others. If he still doesn't want to and has the time, then you remind him that you expect it. And if he still doesn't then he better not be at the top of the list of those you're pushing. If all you do is come to work and do your job and that's it, it's impossible to be a firewall 5, in my book.

Community service isn't about doing something because your boss expects you to and it helps come awards and EPR time, but it's about doing the right thing. It's about helping others because you can.

GET YOUR EDUCATION AND READ

You must take advantage of the educational opportunities presented to you in your life. The Air Force made it extremely easy to get a Community College of the Air Force (CCAF) Associates Degree. There aren't any excuses not to get your Associate's degree. I got my 1st CCAF degree through the normal process of military schools and upgrade training then by CLEP testing the 5 or 6 general education classes required. This was when I was going TDY (temporary duty—work done somewhere away from where you currently live) about 260-280 days a year.

I also didn't waste the opportunity to get my Bachelor's degree when it presented itself. I busted my hump; I earned a degree in three years going to night school all during off duty time, never on duty. I'm an Accounting Major and graduated as Summa Cum Laude. Not bad for a Combat Controller, huh? Along the way I also picked up a CCAF in Instructor of Technology and Military Sciences. I never wasted any opportunity to get more education or become smarter as a person or a professional.

It's a sin when any enlisted person doesn't get their CCAF. The AF paid 75% then 100% tuition up to a certain level. All you had to do was pay for books and spend your time. If you didn't get your CCAF, you were an idiot…the AF gave you so much opportunity and pretty much provided 50% of it to you through normal business.

I would also read a lot of leadership books and would take financial planning and business management courses when I had the opportunity. I would try to stay abreast of all current events I could.

Bottom line: education and knowledge are power. It makes you a better leader and person. Through education comes knowledge and along with that, perspective. The bigger perspective you have, the more informed decisions you'll be able to make. As a leader, you must make informed and timely decisions. They may not be the best, looking back on them (because of hindsight) but they should be the best, based on available information. The more knowledgeable you are, the better decisions you'll be able to make.

YOU ARE A PRODUCT OF YOUR ENVIRONMENT

"When in Rome, do as Romans do." We've all heard this, and when you're in Special Operations this is so true. As Special Tactics we have to be chameleons...able to change according to whom we are working with. Some are truly the best at it, some not so good. In addition to outside units' environments, there are also internal unit environments. For example, the dress and appearance standards are different between units. This is because of the mission. Standards are stricter and less liberal at the Combat Control School than say at the 24 STS. The leadership is less controlling in some units. If most of your troops are mature and experienced, then you don't need to treat them like "regular" military troops. You are able to provide less oversight.

Another way to look at it is if your unit expects you to exceed the standards, you will. If they don't you won't, unless you're like me and some of the other self-motivated people. But for the majority, you're a product of your environment. They'll do what's expected.

If your environment mandates excellence, excellence is what you'll get. Remember the 10% rule: some still won't. If your unit doesn't care about standards, then

41

standards aren't maintained. If your unit "norms" are doing your PT, excellence in work quality and support for community activities, your unit will be a cut above. If your unit's norms don't include excellence, it will probably be a crappy unit.

When the people of Special Tactics were among the regular AF they normally surpassed them in all things. I can't count how many times a Special Tactics member *took wood* (won an award) at PME (Professional Military Education) or was at the top of the class in anything. That's because the "environment" in Special Tactics demands excellence.

Along with being a product of your environment, one must take into account your upbringing, values and motives. These form the individual. Lead dogs will be lead dogs, regardless if in an environment that demands it or not. However, a lot of what you are is determined by the environment you are in.

DO YOUR PT

In our line of work you must be physically fit. We were afforded the opportunity to do Physical Training (PT) during duty hours—it was part of our duty day. PT keeps you mentally, physically and physiologically prepared. As a leader, aside from the personal benefit, your troops need to see you doing PT. A buddy of mine, John MacGarry, told me one day, "*The Air Force pays us to be in shape*." How true he was.

As a leader you need to at least meet any standard the AF or career field throws at you. It sickened me when "headshed" guys (guys in charge) skirted the PT standard or blatantly failed it. But would be the first to scream at you if "their pet peeve" wasn't followed. I could take a chunk of butt anywhere, any time, because my stuff was always squared away. Chewing butt isn't the point. The point is you should do your PT.

Your PT should hit all aspects of fitness. You need to be able to run, force-march with all your gear, swim, lift weights, do calisthenics, be athletic, etc. In essence you need to have strength, endurance and flexibility. Operators are in essence professional athletes...they use their bodies in their profession, and get paid for doing it. It must be taken care of and trained.

Not to oversimplify it but if you were good at doing Obstacle Courses you've met the intent of a PT Warrior. You need everything in the PT toolbox to excel at it and last time I checked no one is timing your 3 mile run in the streets of Baghdad while you're wearing your 2 ounce Nikes and Ranger panties. You need to be agile, flexible, strong, tough, and have endurance…all those needed on an O'Course.

The weapon system in Special Tactics is the man. The man must be prepared to do his job. Part of that job is to be physically fit. You must do your PT.

History is riddled with examples of men who were out of shape and couldn't perform the mission. Consequently, those in shape performed. Don't ever be called a "lump of crap" by another unit when you fail, because you couldn't hump your ruck. No one cares if you normally had more gear than the units you supported, all they care about was did you perform.

PT is another aspect of your character. Ody Dickey said the best way to stay in shape, was to never get out of shape. In our line of work, maintaining PT standards was hard because our schedules often precluded stable PT time. Screw it. Make it happen. Stay in shape and do your PT.

LOYALTY

I don't know if it was my upbringing (Italian American), my Dad (former Marine), my chosen path in life (military), or what, but I am loyal, and cherish loyalty. Loyalty is when you stand by your word because you said you would. Loyalty is not airing your unit's dirty laundry in public. Loyalty is when you help your troop out even if he screwed up, because he's a good troop. Loyalty means supporting your boss in public even if you disagree with him in private. Loyalty is standing by a friend despite him doing something heinous because he's your friend.

People knew whom I was truly loyal to. If you earned my loyalty, there was no better reward. It meant I thought a lot about you. It meant I would do anything for you. It meant you had earned "Sgt V privileges." That means I will overlook certain things because you're such a squared away troop.

Loyalty means I can count on you and you can count on me, no matter what. Not on Mondays or Wednesdays, but every day.

Loyalty also means you can't bad mouth your Country or military in public. We are afforded the rights of free speech, but it doesn't mean you should bad mouth the Man for the sake of free speech.

Loyalty means sticking by your values. When Joker got decked by the Drill Instructor in *Full Metal Jacket*, because he wouldn't take back his response that he didn't believe in the Virgin Mary; the DI, although upset with him, made him the squad leader, "*because Private Joker doesn't have brains, but his got guts, and sometimes guts is enough.*"

Stay loyal.

DISCIPLINE

My father is the most disciplined man I know. After so many years in the military and so much contact with "discipline" I've come to realize what I learned as a kid in his house was all the discipline I needed in life. In essence I spent 18 years in the "military" before my career in the AF even started. My time in the military just perfected or enhanced (whichever way you look at it) my own self-discipline. He grew up in a very strict home. His parents were Italian American, Catholic and his father served in WWII. He is a former Marine. There aren't any "X" Marines, once a Marine always a Marine.

So with his upbringing came discipline, his discipline was a part of our life also. I won't lie to you; it was tough. After 18 years in his house, living under his rules, Air Force basic training was a breeze. Most of my career was easy in the sense it came easy to me, because I worked hard and was disciplined about it. There wasn't anything the Combat Control School instructors could do to me physically, mentally or psychologically that my Old Man hadn't already mastered. Trust me, there was a certain feeling of *elation* when I entered the Air Force and wouldn't have to be controlled by him anymore.

Now it appears I'm bashing my Old Man. On one level I hated his guts, but on another level, I'm the man I am, because of him. I'm proud to say that. He made sure we were doing the things we were supposed to do, when we were supposed to do it. We did PT, (he actually called it that back then), studied hard, worked hard, respected authority, kept our noses clean, and went to Church. All those things you were supposed to do.

I wouldn't say he was a robot, but he was very patterned. He shaved every day; I do also. He made his bed every day; I do also, mostly. He gets up the same time every day; me too. He looked squared away every day for work; so do I. He respected authority; so do I. He did those little things that set people apart from "just average;" so do I.

Discipline is ascribing to a set of moral codes. It means living your life by a certain ideal. It means maintaining the standard and integrity of your profession.

Comrades in Arms

The #1 reason I liked the military so much, was the people I was fortunate enough to meet and become friends with. We volunteered to join this profession of arms and support and defend the Constitution. None of us have a problem with that and proudly do it. We defended our Nation's freedoms as others do to this day and have done in the past. But there's more to it than that. Your buddy next to you means more to you than anything else in the world. At that instant of "deep suck" (a phrase my man Aaron May coined) he is all that matters. Sure you may be putting hot steel on target or hoisting out a downed pilot or whatever your main job was, but the man next to you was the most important thing at that time.

My wife used to give me a hard time about how much time I spent with these men. She even went as far as to say a few choice (negative) words about it. She didn't understand. If you've never been in this position before you just won't understand. But I would do anything for my "brothers." They are that important to me.

Mentoring

Mentoring is when someone takes care of you and your career through advice, suggestions and showing you the way. Mentoring is turning that raw piece of clay into a finished product. It takes time but given the right circumstances, patience and a good mentor, the protégée will become better.

I was mentored by those above me before I knew what the word was. I was mentored by some great men in my life. I have chosen to mentor those around and below me, because I care about them and it's the right thing to do. Once I became a SNCO I also mentored those above me. Now to some that appears wrong, but not to those of us in Spec Ops. The SNCOs are usually smarter and more experienced than anyone else in the game, including the officers. So mentoring was our responsibility.

My mentoring obviously started with my parents. My parents did their best to teach us right from wrong, and were mostly successful. They taught me all those things I mentioned in the discipline section. After I graduated CCS (Combat Control School) great mentors have been there for me. The first was McChord's SCUBA Team Superintendent, MSgt Lee Hughes.

Lee Hughes was the first SNCO I worked for. He is where I started to learn what you were supposed to do when you were in charge. Lee wasn't a PT stud, or one of the chosen ones, but he was our team leader, consequently he was God to us. We called him *Gunny*, out of respect. What I learned from Lee was how to work hard, play hard and take care of your men. Also I learned it is okay to choke out one of your troops if they're screwing up. That's how it was back then. Trust me the troop is better off in the long run and sometimes you need to restate who the Alpha Male is. One of the best things I learned from Lee was how to act like a team. We were on the SCUBA team and believed we were the best at whatever we had to do.

Mark Scholl was my first supervisor when I arrived at the 24 STS. Scrogg, as we called him was one of the smartest guys in CCT and ST I've ever met then and now. Scrogg was a man I respected so much that I would feel bad, like I disappointed him, when he told me I was messing up. This is a common theme. I grew up, starting with my Old Man, learning that it's okay to be told you're messing up and to fix your crap. It seems nowadays people don't like conflict and won't tell it like it is. Scrogg knew everything about everything. He knew the books inside and out and tried to teach me the "rules" of the job, because there are a million and not following some would get your butt in a sling or get someone killed.

Scrogg was a family man, through and through, but when he was TDY he was a different man. Kind of like this little demon that had to get out. He told me once that everyone has his cross to bear and I was his. I knew what he meant and I tapped into his experience and intellect every day. I loved him and was crushed when he died in a training accident in 1992. I used to do the "15-Miler," nicknamed the Scrogg, at the Combat Control School. It was the last physical event at CCS following the FTX (Field Training Exercise—the last objective to graduate CCS). It was 15 miles from the backside of Normandy DZ back to CCS. You had to carry all your gear (ruck, LBE and weapon). I did every single one (I didn't have to do any) during my tenure at CCS solely in honor of Scrogg. I told very few people that up until now. That's the primary reason I did it, because of him. Sure it looked cool when I would be out there hanging with the students, but that wasn't the primary reason, although I hope they took notes how I was leading from the front.

I keep things with me that are important, as some of you may. Scrogg wrote the below paper when he attended the NCO Leadership School some time ago.

I've carried it with me most every day. It's important to me and I know Scrogg would approve of me sharing it with you.

A Journey to Freedom

Man has been searching for FREEDOM since the beginning of time. FREEDOM from the elements and aggression was the initial goal. As mankind advanced, an element arose which presented an even greater danger. Oppression, to gain FREEDOM from the oppressor. A man would have to overcome sizable obstacles and clinging snares in his path.

Our ancestors conquered this trail. Their travels brought them from Asia, Africa, Europe, everywhere. Many forfeited comfortable lifestyles in search of a higher ideal. This continues today. As you read this, a family peers north across the Rio Grande. Their eyes affixed upon the bastion of FREEDOM. The United States of America. The Liberator. The Example.

This luxurious FREEDOM did not come without cost. Heavy withdrawals were made on our checkbook. Lexington and Concord, Valley Forge, and Gettysburg escalate the cost of the journey. Your forefathers paid it. Many believed in this mission so deeply that they contributed their final paycheck. A heavy donation toward the grubstake, which fueled this trip toward the destination, FREEDOM.

Armed conflict was not the only demon, which plagued the traveler. Internal restriction of men and women occurred.

Some people were denied a say in our "Democracy." Through the selfless perseverance of many, this door was breeched and the journey continued.

The journey to FREEDOM is a never-ending trek. The baton is passed from generation to generation. Along the road, the traveler must make sacrifices and be on the lookout for roadblocks, which must be cleared from the trail. Sometimes military strength is required. At other times, just the stoke of your pen.

We carry the baton. FREEDOM rests in our hands. Our parent and grandparents' example taught us to move FREEDOM down the road. It has been a costly venture, but the dividends are great. We must preserve these values and inspire our children to do the same, for the journey to FREEDOM is a never-ending trip.

TSgt Mark Scholl

Scott Fales was one of my Silver Team (best team) superintendents during my tenure at 24 STS. Scott was a PJ (Pararescueman) and one of the first I worked for. To me a SNCO is a SNCO (most of the time) so AFSC (Air Force Specialty Code—your job) shouldn't matter. A key thing I learned from Scottie was to call BS when the situation demanded it. Also, Scottie never asked anything of us that he wouldn't do himself. Scott was also a great teacher about ST stuff. Scott took care of me and let me get away with some transgressions because I proved myself with him and he would support me.

Scott was what I thought a SNCO was supposed to be like…a professional, disciplined soldier. I would spend a lot of time talking to him about my career and unit issues and most everything under the sun. He would selflessly give me his time when I asked. Scottie got wounded in Mogadishu, Somalia in 1993 and while he was wounded was still doing his job: leading from the front. Below is a quote from him that he wrote when he was in the hospital. It's extremely insightful and I carry it with me in my backpack. Wherever that backpack went, Scottie's quote went with me.

WHAT I LEARNED IN THE FIRE FIGHT

*In a firefight life is a series of interrelated instances, your continued existence is determined by inches and nano-seconds. Scenes become snapshots frozen in time, everything in slow motion. The air is void of sound yet you are immersed in ear shattering thunder. All your senses are crisp, adrenaline pumping, your mind screaming. Never forget, this is when **death** watches and waits for his chance to steal your life. Because it's during those instances you are the most **alive!!!***

MSgt Scott Fales
Mogadishu, Somalia, October 1993

Ken Rodriguez was my team leader, director of operations and commander. I loved RZ. He was one of the sharpest, articulate and insightful men I ever had the pleasure to be around. RZ never slacked even though he was busier than any of us ever thought we were. He would do whatever we were doing plus his primary responsibilities.

RZ had a way of talking to me that inspired and motivated me. He took mentoring me as a personal mission. You could tell there were guys that would mentor because they were supposed to and it showed; but RZ truly wanted to, because he cared and made those he did mentor better. RZ always had a kind word for me and my family and wherever our travels took us would ask about my family and my personal life.

RZ led the most professional and competent unit in the AF during Operations ENDURING FREEDOM and IRAQI FREEDOM. He dealt with hardship, heartbreak, and victory; everything war brings with the utmost of professionalism and effectiveness.

Sure there were times when not everyone agreed with him, but you'll never get 100% of the people to agree 100% of the time. That's why they pay us to lead, not to wet nurse everyone, but to get the mission done. But RZ also took care of his people. I've only been counseled by RZ once and I totally deserved it. I said something to him I shouldn't have and he pulled me into a room and kicked me in the backside, built me back up and sent me out the door a new man. It's great when you can be told you screwed up, and then leave without the tension of your boss holding a grudge. I personally would feel bad if I got yelled at or counseled, mainly because I felt I let the guy down, not because I was upset for getting yelled at.

Jack McMullen, or Mad Jack as he is known, was a guy I've been stationed with for about 10 years in different units. Jack was one of my bosses at the Combat Control School. One thing that Jack let me do was let me run the CCS when he could have simply micromanaged me. Jack trusted me to do what I was paid to do…lead men and make stuff happen. I love running things my own way, as most people do, and as long as I met Jack's intent, we were cool.

But along the way I became self-sufficient and was easily able to handle major issues. Now I'm not saying I hadn't handled major issues before, but it's different when you run a unit. When Jack made Chief he recommended to the commander that I be named the next Commandant of the CCS. We were a geographically separated unit at Pope AFB, NC and the commander was at Lackland AFB, TX. It's an E-8 position but I was only an E-7. I was the Commandant of the CCS for my last year all because Jack trusted me and my performance spoke for itself. To be a MSgt and running your own unit is a phenomenal responsibility and privilege. Jack made that happen for me and I'm grateful for the experience.

Jack would spin up (even by his own admission) but if you knew what Jack needed as far as information or action, then he'd stay out of your backside. If he was in your butt, it wasn't a pretty scene. He was a professional butt chewer. When I had the pleasure of his counseling, once again I earned it. But I was a better SNCO after the fact. Which is why he did it, with me anyway. Some guys just chew butt to chew butt, but Jack did it to me more as a mentor.

Jack also forced me to look at things from a bigger perspective. As a sled dog, you only need to worry about your primary job and the normal organization rules, etc, but as a SNCO you need to worry about a lot of other things. You also need to be an example for not only your unit, but also for your base and AF.

Tim Brown, or TB, was another boss of mine and a career long confidant. TB did a lot of that Special Operations stuff that no one knows about, well only a few people. He's been there and done that. He has excelled at every position and job he had. TB, like Lee Hughes, made us work hard but also played hard. TB taught me a lot but one particular thing was to have all your stuff together at all times. You never know when you'll be called to go prosecute the mission.

TB gave me an immense amount of career advice and it all panned out just like he called it. He was a sharp dude. He not only was a very adept operator but was also smart on the ways of the military and admin crap.

TB wasn't a yeller; mainly because he never had to. It wasn't his style. In my time with him, we had a great team and unit. TB just made stuff happen and didn't make a big deal about it. He did what SNCOs are supposed to do...bust their hump, do their jobs and take care of their men.

In my opinion TB was "passed over" for a job I think (as did others) he deserved and our community needed him there. But like the professional he was, he pressed on, filled a new position and made tremendous strides that will positively affect the entire Special Tactics community for years to come. Bottom line: he did his job.

I'm loyal to my unit, AF, country and those men that have earned my loyalty. TB earned my lifelong loyalty. I would call TB on any subject and he would take the time to give me his sage advice. I made very few huge career-affecting decisions without his counsel. It was always emotionless, specific, insightful, and big-picture oriented.

Mike Nazionalle, or "Naz" as we called him, was a Lieutenant at my first unit, and we didn't have a lot of contact but became my team leader at the second unit. He was prior enlisted, so knew the deal (not all do). What Naz did for me was set a good example for the sled dogs. He did most everything right. Now I knew him later on in his career, so my perspective may not be everyone else's; who cares.

Naz was pretty hard core for an officer and showed us how to lead. Naz taught us to never take someone else's side of a story "against" your man until you hear your man's side of it. You can't imagine how often this lesson proved itself out.

I remember when one time I had a team in a foreign country doing that operator stuff and according to the time line they were a little behind schedule. I was in the JOC (the operations hub) and the commander was asking "what the heck?" He actually used a harsher word. Also a certain General was actually in the field observing the op. I explained tactfully to trust the team in the field, there's probably a good reason. Anyway, they were setting up a runway for some other dudes to come in a do their deal, and some local police rolled up on them. Now we had live weapons as they did, but our team did their job, got out of the situation, set up the runway, landed the plane (only a little late) and then exfiled.

The moral of the story is never question your men in the field until you talk to them. The next day, I talked to them and they explained what happened. They did everything they were supposed to. A common tendency is to think the worst, and even though sometimes I do, I try to wait to judge until I talk to my men. This lesson has served me well my entire career.

Naz died in the same training accident as Scrogg and in one instant we lost our team leader, Scrogg, and a sled dog, Mark Lee. It crushed me, but because of Naz's leadership and mentorship our team pressed on and became stronger because of the experience.

I have mentored a lot of men in my day; some may or may not realize it. My mentoring was free. Those true protégées of mine knew I was their mentor. I took a personal interest in their professional lives and watched them grow. Now I don't take total credit for it, but I do hope I had a positive impact.

I am the man I am because of those who've mentored me. They took their time to make <u>me</u> better and for that I'm appreciative.

REINFORCEMENT

If you want to stop a bad behavior or continue a good behavior you need to provide negative or positive reinforcement, respectively. For example, if a guy exceeds the standard, positive reinforcement includes a pat on the back, a little hooyah, a pass, or anything that is perceived as positive by your troop.

If a guy doesn't measure up on a certain task or issue, to stop that behavior you need to use negative reinforcement. This could include a stern yelling to, some BS detail, or some physical labor. Bottom line: you have to express that this behavior must stop.

You can't use positive reinforcement when a guy just meets the standard. For example, giving him a pat on the back for showing up to work on time. He's supposed to do that. You'll lessen the value of the reinforcement if it's used incorrectly. Same thing with the negative reinforcement: you can't rely on the same type or overuse it. It will lose its effect. Your objective is to say with positive reinforcement, I like it, continue and with negative reinforcement, I don't approve, stop it.

You can also reinforce something by your inaction, specifically when a man doesn't measure up. For example, if a guy doesn't show up to work on time and you don't do anything, you've just said it's okay, reinforcing that behavior.

Behavior is learned and subsequently can be changed. To change it you must reinforce it positively or negatively.

THE COMMANDER IN CHIEF

The below excerpt is about President George W. Bush. It was forwarded to me on email to "forward" to everyone else I knew...you guys know those types of emails. Normally I deleted those things thinking they were spam (most were). I didn't forward it...but was one of the few things I actually kept. It points to respect, loyalty, service and leadership. I felt it appropriate to include.

First, an observation. Notice the difference in the salute given by our military men and women as President Bush walks by compared to what they did during the previous administration? Most folks would not notice anything, but those of us who have served in the military see it right away. Next time, watch as President Bush leaves his helicopter or Air Force One. The honor guards salute and face him as he disembarks, then turn their faces towards him as he passes by. They continue to salute his back as he walks away. This kind of salute has not been seen in the previous eight years, though it is customary courtesy to the Commander-in-Chief. You see, soldiers aren't required to turn and face the President as they salute. They are not required to salute his back. They are only required to salute. They can remain face-forward the entire time. And that is what they did during the previous administration. Our soldiers were forced to obey his orders, but they were not forced to respect him. From their salutes, we can surmise that they did not.

The following incident from Major General Van Antwerp provides an insight into this respect. Major General Antwerp is president of the Officers' Christian Fellowship. He lost nearly all his staff when the Pentagon was attacked on September 11th. His executive officer LTC Brian Birdwell was badly burned and in the hospital when President Bush visited him. Our President spent time and prayed with Brian. As he was getting ready to leave, he went to the foot of Brian's bed and saluted. He held his salute until Brian was able to raise his burned and bandaged arm, ever so slowly, in return. The Commander-in-Chief almost never initiates a salute, except in the case of a Congressional Medal of Honor winner. The injured soldier did not have to return the salute. But he did, out of respect to his President …a Soldiers' President.

Congressman JC Watts (R. Oklahoma) said, "Character is doing the right thing when nobody is looking." The nation and world learned some of what our last President did when nobody was looking. In this time of war and danger, I am so grateful to have a President whom the soldiers salute -- fully. On Special Report with Brit Hume, at the close of the show when they normally have some funny *video clip, they showed President Bush and the First Lady on their way to Maine to leave for Camp David for the weekend. As the video starts, the First Lady is leading the way into the helicopter with the spaniel dog on the leash, and the President is right behind her with the Scotty on the leash. As the First Lady entered the chopper, the Marine at the gangway saluted and held his salute. The Scottie the President was walking decided it wanted to sit right when he got to the steps. The President pulled on its leash, but the stubborn Scottie persisted in sitting. The President bent down and scooped up the pooch and entered Marine One. After he entered, the Marine cut his salute and returned to the position of attention. Moments later the President reemerged from the helicopter and out onto the steps. The Marine was standing at attention, head and eyes straight ahead. The President leaned over and tapped him on the left arm. The startled Marine turned his body toward the President and received his returned salute!*

I was so impressed by this true act of respect for our military people by our President! He really does get it. Most any other person of his stature would have just continued his journey, disregarding the neglected return salute. Not George W. Bush. He is earning the respect of the military community, not expecting it -- as most have and would.

President George W. Bush, the man who admitted to having a drinking problem in younger years, and whose happy-go-lucky lifestyle led him to mediocre grades in college and an ill-fated oil venture. Who mangled syntax, and whose speaking mis-steps became known as "Bushisms." He came within a hair's breadth of losing the election in November.

On September 11, he was thrust into a position only known by the likes of Roosevelt, Churchill, Lincoln, and Washington. The weight of the world was on his shoulders, and the responsibility of a generation was on his soul. So President George W. Bush walked to his seat at the front of the National Cathedral just three days after two of the most impressive symbols of American capitalism and prosperity virtually evaporated. When the history of this time is written, it will be acknowledged by friend and foe alike that President George W. Bush came of age in that cathedral and lifted a nation off its knees. In what was one of the most impressive exhibitions of self-control in presidential history, President George W. Bush was able to deliver his remarks without losing his resolve, focus, or confidence. God's hand, which guided him through that sliver-thin election, now rested fully on him. As he walked back to his seat, the camera angle was appropriate. He was virtually alone in the scene, alone in that massive place with God, just him and the Lord.

Back at his seat, George H. Bush reached over and took his son's hand. In that gesture his father seemed to say, "I wish I could do this for you, son, but I can't. You have to do this on your own." President George W. Bush squeezed back and gave him a look of peace that said, "I don't have to do it alone, Dad. I've got Help." What a blessing to have a professing Christian as President.

Please take a moment after you read this to "pray for him." He truly does have the weight of the world on his shoulders. Pray that God will sustain him and give him wisdom and discernment in his decisions. Pray for his protection and that of his family. And after you have prayed, send this to everyone on your e-mail list. Our President needs Christians, Democrats and Republicans alike, to be praying for him.

FEEDBACK

Feedback is a two-way street. It's most effective when it's specific, timely and constructive. Some of those that outrank others don't freely accept feedback. Well I do and did. If you don't know what effect you're having on your people, how do you know if you're successful or not? Some people would say, "who cares?" Well as a modern day leader you should care what your people think.

To take a step back, you need to provide your folks feedback on how they're doing. They deserve it and it's mandated in some circles. It's been proven when you tell your folks your expectations performance will improve.

And vice-versa; your folks should be allowed to let you know how you're doing. As long as it is specific and constructive. I have no fear of being told I'm messed up. There are a few rules when giving feedback.

Feedback should timely follow the issue in reference. "Remember how good you did on that project last month?" doesn't cut it. By being timely the individual immediately associates the feedback with the issue and it has a more profound effect. Feedback needs to be specific. "You're an outstanding troop." This isn't specific. Try, "I appreciate how you invented that new flux capacitor process increasing our efficiency by 100%." If negative, "Quit screwing up!" may not be the most appropriate specific feedback, although I've used it and it works. Negative feedback also needs to be specific. For example, "Get your stupid hair cut now, or I'll do it myself!"

Feedback also needs to touch on the future. When you give timely, specific feedback ensure to show your appreciation and how you expect the same thing in the future. It sort of says, great job, I appreciate it, keep doing it.

Air Force Promotion System

People would ask me all the time if I liked the Air Force promotion system. I wouldn't say I was a huge proponent or opponent. I knew the rules and couldn't think of a better way of doing it...see "rules" section. One thing was that it was a known entity. You knew what you needed to do to get promoted. I knew the way and I guess to a certain extent was pretty good at getting promoted. So in a sense I was a proponent of it. I knew the deal and busted my hump to get promoted. There is no honor in being a "career" SSgt. I've heard every excuse in the world, "I focus my off duty time on my family." "I don't want the extra responsibility." "I don't have time." "The promotion system is crap." "I didn't know I was testing this year." All are just that: excuses.

I never apologized why I studied and made rank. I wanted to be a higher rank. I wanted to be in charge. I thought I was smarter and better than the next guy so I deserved to be in charge. Besides, I wanted the extra money. I don't deny I liked the extra money that came with increased promotion. You can't make positive changes or positively influence people as a SSgt except on a small scale.

There were those that I started to outrank early in my career that were older than me and had more time in the military than me. And it only became more pronounced as I got older. That caused them some undue stress. Lead, follow or get the heck out of the way. Don't get upset because I tried to make things better for my family or myself. Or try to bring me down by talking crap to me because now I outrank you.

The only reason you didn't get promoted is because of the guy you look at in the mirror. One of my favorites was when this one dude told me the only reason I made rank is because I was a good tester. That's almost like saying the only reason Joe Montana was MVP was because he was a better winner than anyone else. Duh! Obviously, there is more to the promotion system than testing. Testing is part of it and if you ignore that part, because it's uncool or whatever, then don't whine when you don't make rank.

Bottom line: no matter what profession you are in, figure out the way to get promoted, master it, then get promoted. You'll have more say in things and the pay is better.

THE WARRIOR

Remember those old Army commercials…"A Soldier never takes the easy way out." Some would say it's easy to be hard; it's hard to be smart. Both have merit. But what does it mean to be a warrior? What is it that makes a warrior? Why are warriors a cut above everyone else? Through training, experience and goal achievement you gain a certain amount of "can do attitude." A warrior doesn't let obstacles get in his way. A warrior can deal with adversity. A warrior makes things happen and smiles about it. A warrior may hate to run but does it anyway because he's supposed to and still kicks butt. A warrior goes into harms way because it's the right thing to do and his buddies are with him doing the same thing.

I can't count how many times I've heard people whine about stupid stuff. I couldn't believe how many people wrote in to the *AF Times* or *Airman Magazine* complaining about some subject they read or saw. One of my favorites was when there were some pictures of PJs in a publication, doing that cool guy stuff. Then about a week or two later there was a letter from some idiot that said he couldn't believe one of the PJs had his Aircrew Wings upside down on his uniform. Well what the dummy didn't realize was they were

Military Freefall Wings and trust me, were properly configured.

This points to a couple of issues. Get your act together when you try to call a warrior out and get a life.

Back to the warrior. Warriors don't complain because their Commander wants to do PT in the cold and rain, they relish it. They think it's another way to train and show their mettle. Warriors say "roger that" when they get off a helo and their team leader retasks them for another mission, so after they load up on ammo, chow, batteries and water they press on. Because that's what warriors do: they press on, no matter what.

Warriors don't show weakness. Warriors are tough in body, mind and soul. Warriors don't tell their boss why they didn't do something they were supposed to. They also don't tell their boss why they suck at running or anything else for that matter. They fix it, plain and simple.

Warriors don't tell their boss how someone else is screwing up, to cover up their own screw ups. Warriors lead from the front. Warriors are your golden geese, they are you're stallions, you're sled dogs. Take care of them.

Warriors are the backbone of your unit. They're the guys you lean on, because they can take it. Your loyalty to your warriors is returned with their loyalty. Warriors can dig deep when they have to. Whatever you think about a warrior negatively is irrelevant. It doesn't matter whether you're right or wrong about a warrior's character. That is also irrelevant. If you aren't a warrior, you can't comment on them.

Warriors have courage. They may be afraid or scared of something, and still do it. They do it because they're warriors. Warriors have guts, spine and heart.

When a buddy (we'll call him TT, along with another bad dude we'll call Sam) kicked the heck out of Northern Iraqi troops in OIF (the war in Iraq), he came out of the field after being employed in bad-guy land for over 3 months. When he walked in the STOC (operations center), we said "hey" and he immediately asked what was his next mission. That's a warrior.

OFFICERS

There is a friend of mine who was prior enlisted and now is an officer. I think she's pretty squared away, and respect a lot of what she says except for one thing. I told her one of my responsibilities was to mentor our young CGOs (lower ranked officers); to make sure they learn from me and the other SNCOs in the unit.

Her immediate retort was it's impossible to mentor an officer because I don't outrank them. Wrong! Ask any Spec Ops SNCO and he'll say he mentors his team leader, his XO (executive officer), DO (director of operations), Commander, whatever. That's how it's done.

You know why it's done that way: because we know more and have experienced more. It behooves young officers to Ranger Assist (stick close to and emulate) their behind to a good SNCO and learn the ropes.

Here's my theory: if we don't make good Lieutenants and Captains, officers will become lousy Commanders. If you see a good Commander he probably came across one or more good SNCOs and learned from them.

It's not bad when an officer takes the advice of a SNCO; it's a sign of respect and actually it's smart. So when I say I've mentored some officers in my life, it means I tried to make them better, consequently making the unit, career field and AF better.

Good officers are good to have, and often times mandatory. They are the ones paid to do that management stuff like justify budgets, articulate positions, etc, even though some SNCOs do the same thing. But when you're in a room negotiating an important issue and the other guy brings a Major, you need a Major also, not a Technical Sergeant. Unless that Tech is Mike "LA" Lamonica. More on that later.

Some times you have to remind the "O's" (officers) that their job is "beans, bullets, care and feeding" and not being a sled dog. A good officer ensures his men are capable of taking care of everything. He should take care of funding, training priorities, admin stuff, etc. An officer doesn't have to be the best air traffic controller or trauma medic; he needs to ensure the best one is available to do the mission.

Officers still have to be competent in whatever their AFSC (their job) is. If they don't know crap about Terminal Air Control (killing bad guys with Airpower), how can they articulate the right tool for the job? But the day a flight commander is rocking the mike and a sled dog is available, something is wrong. An officer must lead and manage.

Teach your officers the right thing to do and have them do the right things. They'll become better men and your unit will be better.

Patriotism

I am a Patriot. I love my country and love the military and love the ideals we stand for. Along the way in my career I realized I was a crier. I'd be at home watching patriotic, inspirational or feel good movies and all of a sudden I'd be leaking like a sieve. I used to try and hide it, thinking it was unmanly. I used to cry at ceremonies or change of commands or retirements. It didn't matter, if it had something to do with us kicking someone's butt or Rocky getting up one last time or Bruce Willis taking it for the team in *Armageddon* I'd be there, goose bumps and all.

Now patriotism isn't about crying. I think crying is a byproduct of pride and emotion. I used to not care about some dude's retirement, but along the way, I went to almost every single one I could. It's important. Like Robert Redford said in *The Last Castle*, "*Every man is a good man after 30 years.*" Retirements are a celebration of a man's career. It should be made public…here stands a man that volunteered to serve his country. Some obviously do it better than others, but bottom line: to have done it takes more of something than most people have.

Patriotism is being proud to salute your flag. Patriotism is standing at attention when retreat (flag ceremony at the end of the duty day) is playing when some are ducking into cars and buildings. Patriotism is not badmouthing your country. Patriotism is taking off your hat at a sporting event when the National Anthem is being played. Patriotism is thanking those veterans who did what we do, only a long time ago. Patriotism is saying, "I'm an American."

"Vinnie you're starting a new STS; pick your first 10 guys."

I've often toyed with the idea that if the Man asked me to start a new unit, whom would I pick? Essentially they'd be the top of the career field. Now the below list isn't all-inclusive but includes the truly best CCT/PJ operators I've ever worked with. They had what I thought was essential to being a good leader, operator or man. Some great guys would be on the 11-50 list, but these are my top 10.

This list doesn't include those dudes that were older or outranked me, although there are a large number of those that would obviously be on my team.

The first is **Mike "LA" Lamonica**. LA is a paisan and I've known him since early on in my career. We've been stationed with each other on numerous occasions. LA is a consummate professional. He is one of the sharpest operators I know. LA knows everything about everything. He is a phenomenal mentor to his men. He is a terrific leader whose style worked with most men. LA would never ask anyone to do anything that he hadn't, wouldn't or couldn't do.

LA's name ends in vowel so automatically we saw eye to eye on a lot of issues. We didn't agree 100% of the time on all things but he was one guy that I didn't need to spend hours explaining my vision or intent to.

LA was also a true patriot. He knew the right things to do. LA led from the front in two wars and countless other times. LA was extremely competent in everything he did. And if he thought he was lagging in a certain area (not often) he'd take it upon himself to buff up.

LA has character. When we was on his way from one unit to the next, he could have left when he was supposed to but instead volunteered to stay longer to help the one he was leaving get through a major inspection. Of course they smoked it. During that time, 9/11 occurred and as in most military units on that day, it was hectic. LA volunteered to stay and keep the unit on the right track. Then shortly following that, he deployed to battle where he and his unit were a huge success. He didn't need to stay at the previous unit as long as he did, but felt it was his duty. That's character.

Rex Freriks is in my top 10 also. Rex is a man you can count on, no matter what. I can't count how many times he helped me when he didn't have to. His competence is virtually unrivaled. He is a true American who lives his life by high ideals. Rex and I ran the "NCO Mafia" back in the day and he was an honorable "street lieutenant."

I know that sounds corny but if you don't know, you can't bust on it. And trust me, most people don't know. They have no idea. Anyway, Rex made stuff happen on sheer determination and an unstoppable work ethic.

There is also that handful of men virtually cut from the same cloth. These guys are the kings of making stuff happen. They have loyalty, guts, maturity, discipline, character, competence, and commitment. It would be an injustice to not mention them.

Part of my top 10 would include: **Kyle Stanbro, Todd Lynch, Keith Edwards, Saleem Ali, Bob "Kiwi" Jeeves, Joe O'Keefe, Billy White, Steve Cast, Aaron May, Tony Travis** and **Wes Brooks.**

Since this is the second edition; there are two dudes that must me added to my top 10. They are **Trey Free** and **Ray Colon-Lopez.**

So I can't count to 10. These guys are the best of the best. They have proven themselves time and time again. I can't tell you how much each of them mean to me and they probably don't even know that they mean that much to me. Bottom line: these men would be unstoppable and are in their current units.

Any time someone makes a list, others invariably question the validity of it. Mainly because they aren't on it, or that someone is they don't like. Well it's my book and these guys are on it and I didn't forget anyone that should be on it. Remember, they're my top 10, except I can't really count to 10.

Goal Setting

You must know where you want to go or you'll never get there. To get past mediocrity or being average you need goals. Goals should be specific although some of my goals were ambiguous or some times intangible.

I carry a list of goals with me in my Day Runner. I updated my list periodically, especially after I achieved a particular goal. Some were obvious: Make rank, weigh a certain amount, attain a certain amount of liquid wealth, etc. I believe your goals will be achieved more readily if they are written down and referred to often, sort of like a contract.

I believe some people's goals weren't specific enough or lofty enough. And yet a lot of people appeared to not have goals at all. I would know this when I'd ask them in passing or in more formal feedback situations. If you can't spew a handful of specific goals out when asked you don't have any or you couldn't articulate them on the spot.

Sure, some people wanted to keep them a secret, and I believe this is to avoid embarrassment if not attained. Another reason I believe is that they lack confidence in themselves. I'm the most confident person I know. I believe if I put my mind and body toward anything I would accomplish it.

Not just individuals, but also organizations need goals. Organizations need to say: Here is what we're going to do this year. In the military a lot of your goals were determined by a higher authority but there was still a huge amount of opportunity to get things done and make things happen.

Set goals to reach your goals.

Motivation

Motivation is an amazing concept. According to Webster *motivate* means: To provide with an incentive or motive. Motive means: An impulse, as an emotion, desire, or physiological need, acting as incitement to action. Some people are by their very nature "motivating." What I take from that is a simple action and reaction or cause and effect. Something is done to someone that causes that person to do something else. There must be a conscious act to do something after a motivating speech. I agree the motivating speech, person, or act may be a catalyst pushing a person to do something but they are two separate actions.

Can a person actually be "motivated?" I think the motivator provides the environment, positive attitude, or vision of the future and the person then decides to undertake what the motivator was instilling.

For example, Vince Lombardi was regarded as a phenomenal motivator. But I believe that all he did was provide an environment and a vision. He inspired his players to the point that they'd do anything for him; they respected him that much. Forrest Gregg said, "*When Coach Lombardi said 'sit down' we didn't bother looking for a chair.*" But bottom line, they made the conscious effort to do what he asked. Vince Lombardi was still Vince Lombardi even if his motivation didn't have the desired effects on all his players.

When I was an instructor and inevitably ran the Combat Control School, we established a disciplined environment and demanded a lot out of our students. Our students, for the most part, would do anything we asked, mainly because of the power and authority we had over them. I had some very motivating instructors. But to truly get through an arduous situation, whether it's a school, a run, an impossible task, whatever, required individual effort.

Sure I've given some pretty motivational speeches in my life but the act of getting to the next step wholly belonged to the receiver of the motivation. Did I give them a nudge? I'm sure. Did I provide them the environment and vision? Definitely.

Do I do what I do because of who I am or Who I am is why I do what I do

I believe the answer is both. I've thought about this for years. And why I arrived at the answer both is because I've lived it. My Dad used to tell me leaders lead. I'm a leader and have always been one. Something as simple as being the quarterback in virtually every pickup football game in my life. That and I can chuck a football pretty good.

I've taken a lead role in every phase of my life. Whether I was the ranking guy or not was irrelevant. If something needed to be done, I did it. If something needed to be done and took more than me to do, I got the people to help me do it. When I needed to fulfill a responsibility I did it; I didn't have to be told.

That's why I believe I do what I do because of who I am. I'd be "Vinnie" whether I was in CCT or not.

But because I was a leader I would do things after a while because I thought I was supposed to do them. You do that enough (it takes years) and eventually you do it without even thinking of it. For example, being the first guy to work was something I did, because I thought that was what I was supposed to do. Before I knew it, that's just what I did. So in essence: Who I am is why I do what I do.

Do you believe leaders are born or made? This is another "chicken and egg" question. I believe I was born the way I am (sort of hard-wired if you will) but was trained or made because of my upbringing and my military career. I am a product of my environment.

You are what you are. I am a leader and do what I do because of who I am and who I am is why I do what I do. The two are inseparable.

POWER

There are many forms, types and laws of power. In PME (Professional Military Education) we are taught a lot of them. Even if you didn't get a formal lesson on types of power, you could probably figure out one or a few that are on the list. Power is plainly and simply the ability to get things done for you or your organization.

The most obvious type of power in the military is your rank. You can do a lot as an SSgt but not as much as a Chief. When you make Chief, now you can fix all those issues you said you would if that day ever came. It's a sin when you don't.

I was making stuff happen because of the power I wielded as a SSgt. But more importantly, I didn't need to wait until I was a Chief to make some real change and make real things happen. Some people will never have rank power, for a number of reasons. Rank is good to lean on when you need it, but overuse will dilute its power. Your subordinates can also use your rank. Some people wouldn't mess with my troops even if they weren't doing what they were supposed to be doing, simply because I was their boss. Now I'm not saying that's right or wrong, I'm just saying that's how it was. Or they could say, "Sgt V says…," even if I didn't say a thing.

Another type of power is your personality. If you are liked, respected, feared, whatever, you have a certain amount of power. In my opinion, I had a personality that carried me a far way with "most" people. I have a certain amount of charisma and some people would be drawn to me because of it. Apparently most people liked me and that carried with it a certain amount of juice.

You can also exert some juice due to your expertise in your job or a particular task. I was pretty good at the technical aspects of my job. As a sled dog I had an insatiable appetite for knowledge and experience and still do. I would study different pieces of gear that came in and try to master different job skills. Before I knew it, I was a pretty good Combat Controller…essentially I knew my stuff. If you aren't an expert in an area you need to become one or capitalize on strengths in other areas. I heard Andrew Carnegie has something like this on his headstone: *"Here lies a man who hired men that were smarter than him."* A leader doesn't have to be the smartest guy in the shop. But he needs to be the smartest on how to get everyone to work together.

Earned power I believe is a combination of all your other powers. You get it from years of making things happen. One way earned power is recognizable is when you are asked for by name by other units or senior leaders to do some task or fill some position. Nothing is as powerful as earned power, it sort of precedes you. You must also continue to earn your power; you can't rest on your laurels.

Use your different forms of power to effect things.

The following is a paper I did while at the Air Force Senior Noncommissioned Officer Academy. I thought it appropriate to include here. Please excuse the formality, that's how I had to write it in class.

SITUATIONAL LEADERSHIP AND POWER AT THE COMBAT CONTROL SCHOOL

1. If you don't have "juice" you can't lead. If you don't have power, you don't have what it takes to lead. As senior noncommissioned officers mastery of situational leadership and power will give you and your unit the best opportunity to excel and get the most out of your people. I will explore the relationship between situational leadership and power through some personal examples during my tenure at the Combat Control School (CCS). I will introduce a subordinate of mine and show how he handled the numerous issues at the CCS through effective use of situational leadership and power bases. Who was that subordinate?

2. When I was the Commandant of the CCS my #2 man was the Director of Operations, Technical Sergeant Michael Lamonica. I couldn't have asked for a better #2 man in the entire career field. I've known Mike since 1987 and we both have essentially the same styles of leadership and way of handling things. We both utilize situational leadership and our power bases well and actually have very diverse and broad power bases. In our perspective, we lead by example... from the front. We realized early, to get high standards you must expect high standards. This carried over into our tenure at the CCS.

3.   Our objective was to get our students to do as well as possible as quickly as possible. In essence get them to Readiness Level 4 (R4) as soon as possible. Every student walks in with some readiness. Depending on the task they could be either an R1 through an R4. Overall our students were motivated, disciplined, eager to learn, physical studs. From day one of training we would evaluate their readiness level to assess where they were.

4.   In a school environment a lot of directive behavior or Situational Leadership Style 1 (S1) was required because of the students' readiness level.   Blanchard in his book *Leadership and the One Minute Manager*, expresses there are four basic leadership styles: 1-Directing or Telling, 2-Coaching or Selling, 3-Supporting or Participating and 4-Delegating.   (Blanchard: 30)   Mike and I used all the Situational Leadership styles and power bases at our disposal. The most obvious was the coercive.   Hersey and Blanchard in their book *Management of Organizational Behavior*, state there are seven power bases including: coercive, connection, reward, legitimate, referent, information, and expert.   (Hersey and Blanchard: 228-231)

5.   We demanded a lot from our young warriors. Most of the time they would perform but when they didn't they knew

the consequences. It could take the form of a real bad "butt" chewing, paperwork, pushups or points. Students have 100 points when they arrive; they need 70 to graduate. A student could lose a point for a uniform violation or five points if his weapon was more than an arm's reach away. The quicker a class/student's readiness level rose the quicker our style would change.

6. I created an instructor-student relationship to one that was professional and enhanced learning. Effective situational leadership was the order of the day. The students' behavior would determine our leadership style. Hersey, an organizational theorist in his article Situational Leadership, asserts problems develop when we as leaders have not accurately diagnosed what people need by way of direction. We tend to make decisions on leadership style based on how we like to be led, instead of how the person needs to be led. (www.triangle.org) Mike and I could handle every student issue brought to our attention through our connection power. As members of the First Sergeant Council and Top III Organization we knew most people on base and could make things happen with a phone call.

7. I delegated a huge amount of authority to Mike. I vary rarely left S4 with Mike. His legitimate power coupled with the power I delegated to him allowed him to run the day-to-day operations of the CCS including the overall supervision of the instructor staff. His task and relationship behavior on any subject and to either instructor or student was rarely questioned because of his legitimate authority. As said earlier we expected a lot out of our students. When they exceeded the standards we rewarded them. Mike's methods were often the most effective. He could ride a student or class unmercifully, only to reward them a day later for doing a great job. The students realized they would rather deal with Mike's reward power instead of his coercive power. He wielded all of his power bases with such outstanding situational leadership; it increased the effectiveness of his instructors and more importantly the performance of the students. Mike and I had huge legitimate power; but Mike's referent power was what made him really effective.

8. Students liked being around him. They wanted to excel for him and were mad at themselves when they let him down. Mike's been there done that. Students like being around a guy who can back up a day's lesson with real-world experience. Mike is a master communicator. He always provided constructive feedback. Whether it was positive or negative conditional strokes, he was always constructive. He would always pass on information that concerned the CCS or the students specifically. If the students needed to know something he'd initiate or they'd ask and he'd have the answer. Like his referent power, his expert power was unmatched.

9. He was one of my best instructors because of his vast experience and ability to relay it in terms students could understand. I realize at an AFSC-awarding course, everyone appears to be an expert to students; however, Mike was the most knowledgeable of anyone on my staff. If he didn't know from memory he'd know exactly where to find the answer. He made numerous decisions based solely on his expertise that enhanced training or ensured a sticky situation went smooth. As our students increased their skills, knowledge and abilities Mike would adjust his leadership style. He had an amazing knack to immediately switch between styles depending on the situation. He could use S4 with one of his instructors and immediately transition to S1 with the students and vice versa. His ability to use his phenomenal situational leadership coupled with his use of his power bases, ensured the CCS was a professional and disciplined organization and our students some of the most well prepared.

10. A look at Mike's tenure at the CCS is like looking at a leadership textbook. Mike adeptly used all of the power bases. He would use coercive, connection, reward, legitimate, referent, information and expert. He would adjust his leadership style from an S1 through an S4 depending on his subordinates' readiness levels. His excellent use of both situational leadership styles and power proved his outstanding effectiveness. As senior noncommissioned officers mastery of situational leadership and power will give you and your unit the best opportunity to excel and get the most out of your people. Remember that our guys can be in combat a little after they graduate, we need the juice to lead them, the power that says, "follow me."

What the Senior "E" does for a Unit

A lot of people would ask me what my job was as the Senior Enlisted Manger. I would explain the book answer to them, and most would still not get it. In Special Tactics the Senior "E" whether a SMSgt or CMSgt would do virtually the same things except they may be in different sized units.

First and foremost the Senior "E" takes care of manpower issues. If it pertains to personnel he's involved. Now this doesn't take away from what the First Sergeant does; they should be working together as a team. The only difference in ST compared to what I perceive in <u>most</u> regular AF units: the Senior "E" was the Alpha Male, not the Shirt.

The Senior "E" ensures there is an order of merit to your sled dogs and lead dogs. He ensures the right ones are being recognized and pushes the lead dogs out front.

He also handles those "special projects" that your boss (the commander) needs you to take care of. This could be anything from ensuring the unit was ready to go to battle, facility projects, preparing for a major inspection, basically handling those big issues that don't really fall in the purview of anyone else.

Now Senior "E's" handle a myriad of issues aside from the aforementioned few. Bottom line: they handle personnel, programs, and processes.

What does the Senior "E" really do? Depending on the unit you're in, and the commander you work for, below are a few examples I've experienced or know happen.

First, you take care of your commander. You don't let him take any heat that you can square away. You ensure he is kept "untouchable." You're sort of his "Chief of Staff" or "Trusted Agent" if you will. If an issue can get bloody (figuratively) or embarrassing or whatever, you handle it. If it gets messed up, you ensure the Old Man doesn't get the blame for it. Well, unless he truly is the blame for it and <u>needs</u> to be moved on. Then of course you help move him along.

The Senior "E" handles the scut work for the boss. He may not even ask you to do it, or imply for you to do it or intend for you to do it. Regardless, you handle it. If you don't handle it personally you get one of your lead dogs to do it.

In some units you provide the compass or direction. Sure the Commander is in charge and the Director of Operations runs the operational side of the house, but the Senior "E" should be looked to as to what the unit should be doing. Some would say he actually runs the unit. Now if your commander is secure in his manhood and trusts/respects his Senior "E" then this won't be a problem. A majority of issues in a unit are affected and effected by the enlisted and because of that the Senior "E" handles it.

It's not a "power grab;" that's just the way it is. I knew my Commander was the boss and didn't step on his toes. If anything, I ensured his policies were upheld and would support him, regardless if I disagreed with him. Commanders don't root around in any backsides if it comes to that, and more often than not it wouldn't. But because of that it would appear the Senior "E" ran the joint. The commander is the boss. He should worry about bigger things not why Airman Shmedlab was late to work.

The Senior "E" keeps the unit going in the right direction and doing the right thing. He should be the all knowing or at least know where to get the information. His hands should be in nearly everything to at least a level he can positively affect it if required. Bottom line: the Senior "E" makes things happen.

Is It Better to be Loved or Feared?

An often-quoted book, *The Prince*, by Niccolo Machiavelli addresses this issue. Plus I've heard it referenced in other areas. Before I get to that, *The Prince* is referenced, quoted, and talked about in a lot of leadership books I've read. Essentially, it's a gift from Machiavelli to the Magnificent Lorenzo Di Piero de' Medici. It is based on his long experience around men of importance and deals with all those subjects a man in a leadership position would deal with.

It was written during the Italian Renaissance so it definitely needs to be related to modern time, but most of the concepts and theories are timeless. Anyway, he addresses the issue if it's better for a prince to be loved or feared. Machiavelli starts by saying "*every prince ought to desire to be considered clement and not cruel. Nevertheless he ought to take care not to misuse this clemency.*"

Most people, as I did, would probably answer that it's better to be both. Machiavelli continues "*it is difficult to unite them in one person, it is much safer to be feared than loved, when, of the two, either must be dispensed with.*" Also, "*love is preserved by the link of obligation which, owing to the baseness of men, is broken at every opportunity for their advantage; but fear preserves you by a dread of punishment which never fails."*

He goes on to explain that a prince should inspire fear in a way that if he isn't loved, he avoids hatred. He can always do this by not illegally taking his subjects' property, their women or killing unnecessarily.

Machiavelli finishes, *"men loving according to their own will and fearing according to that of the prince, a wise prince should establish himself on that which is in his own control and not in that of others; he must endeavour only to avoid hatred."*

When I reflect on my past and present I know I've been loved, feared and hated. All true leaders have in my opinion. It may point to the 10%...no matter what you do, some people won't be happy. Your techniques and style have a lot to do with how people perceive and react to you. Your style (as some times mine doesn't) may not work in all situations. Style flexibility and situational leadership are key. As a leader grows and matures he builds a reputation throughout his career. He is known as certain type of person.

As I've said, I initially and still sometimes wish to be both loved and feared. But when I think of the instances where I've had the most effect, I obviously wasn't hated, but respected. A good leader gets the job done through people and has his people still motivated. To ensure your people remain motivated and willing to make stuff happen a leader can't be hated.

What I get out of Machiavelli's point is if you're too loved, your men will, over time, find a way to walk on you. If you are feared you sort of keep them in line because they know the consequences. The danger is obviously if your people are always afraid will they have the initiative, creativity or willingness to go above and beyond; probably not. But out of this, you can't become hated because you have no way to motivate either through love or fear.

Bottom line: ensure to become respected and depending on the situation and, the people in question and how they react to you, it will either be out of love or fear.

Qualities of a Leader

Below is a list of qualities I find important in a leader. This list is not all-inclusive.

- Character: This is the foundation of a man. Gotta have it. It's not made during adversity; it's revealed. See previous character section.

- Loyalty: You must have loyalty to your men, your boss, your unit, AF, and country. Loyalty means you can lean on me, count on me, and trust me.

- Commitment: See previous commitment section.

- Integrity: You must be honest. You must be faithful and stand by your word. You must uphold the morals and values of your profession.

- Courage: Dealing with adversity. Being afraid but still making it happen. Having some guts.

- Strength: Physical, mental and moral. Be a pillar; be the rock; show you can also be leaned on.

- Persistence: Don't ever give up. Press on with your deal. Never quit. Remain focused and on course.

- Telling it like it is…speaking your mind: You're paid to address problems. Who cares if you step on toes and ruffle some feathers? If you're right say it's messed up.

- Good Listener: Your folks make the mission happen. They're smart and experienced. Value what they have to say. Give them a say in things. You can't do it alone; you need to listen to them.

- Energetic: Never stop, don't take a break, and don't rest on your laurels. Take action, keep moving, make things happen.

- Decisive: Make a decision and stick to it. Don't waffle. Lead, follow, or get the heck out of the way.

- Adaptability: Every situation is different. Adapt to your environment. Learn from your mistakes; work on your weaknesses.

- Resourceful: Make things happen. Don't let obstacles stand in your way. Figure it out even if you aren't trained specifically on it.

- Competence: See previous competence section.

- Charisma: Have a personality. Have a presence. Be at least likable.

- Heart: Dig deep when you need to. Have some guts.

What the Air Force Means to Me

The following paragraphs are a speech I gave on September 18, 2002 when the 352 SOG celebrated the AF Birthday.

Good afternoon, my name is SMSgt Paul Venturella and I am the Senior Enlisted Manager for the 321st Special Tactics Squadron. It is with great privilege I stand here today to tell you what the Air Force means to me.

What does the Air Force mean to me? That's a broad question with many answers...or does it only have one?

The Air Force means to me many things...When I was at the 24th Special Tactics Squadron we went to Desert Storm as some of you may have. We went to defend freedom, democracy and our national interests. But why did Staff Sergeant Venturella go...why did I go? I went because I was told to, because it was my duty and because my teammates went.

What does the Air Force mean to me...it means standing by my teammates' sides because they'll do the same for me. It means loyalty to my brothers, my unit and my Air Force even if I think they're wrong. It means doing the right thing when no one is watching. It means leading by example...from the front.

During Desert Storm we hunted for and destroyed Iraqi Scuds. We were on the front lines of Desert Storm. We were a small Joint Special Operations Task Force in a large US contingent. We did our jobs and we did them well. Each one of us knew our role. That's what the Air Force means to me.

When we went to Haiti for Operation UPHOLD DEMOCRACY I was part of a small Special Tactics team that ran Port au Prince International Airport. We were on the first wave of hundreds that entered that small country. We ran the airport for 27 non-stop hours until relieved by conventional forces.

We started the operation to liberate that country and install democracy and self-sufficiency. Why did we go? Because we were told to. Because it was the right thing to do. Because our teammates were going.

What does the Air Force mean to me…it means exceeding the standards. It means discipline and silent professionalism. It means character, competence and commitment. It means we have a higher calling.

Recently our Air Force…our AFSOC, lost 10 warriors in an accident in Puerto Rico. Special Tactics lost three of its best. One of those was one of my best friends, a former troop, one of my go to guys at the Combat Control School and a brother. TSgt Chris Matero, or MO as we called him was the total package. He did everything right. He was the perfect troop. I tried to lead by example...from the front. To be that example for MO. To be that example for all of my guys.

I still do that today. I tried to be his rock. He could lean on me, I was there for him. And along the way he became my rock. The one I could lean on. What does the Air Force mean to me...

It means Chris Matero, it means Jason Cunningham, it means John Chapman, and it means MSgt Gilbertson and his maintenance crew on the USS LaSalle. That crew was full of great Americans. As most of you know MH-53s are temperamental. Gilby's crew would spend hours inside the guts of those old birds. I truly believe they're most happy covered head to toe in grease. Happy when everyone is asleep working their magic so tomorrow when a guy like Joe Becker or Shawn Leroy gets up in the morning...they can say, sir...she's ready for you.

Why do I do what I do? Because that's what I think I'm supposed to do. Because that's what I was trained to do. Because that's how my parents raised me. Because that's my job...and I'm in the military.

What does the Air Force mean to me?

It means thanking the Security Forces troop for doing his job during the nasty and typical English weather for 12-

16 hours at a pop. It means showing your troops the way, when they don't know. It means giving your commander constructive advice because you've done it your way before… and it worked. It means rechecking something for the third time because the IG will check twice.

What does the Air Force mean to me…In a word it means Service. Service to my unit, my SOG, my Air Force and my country. As we celebrate our Air Force's 55th Birthday, reflect on what it means to you. Remember we took an oath. We all volunteered to serve and those past our 1st enlistment we did it again, again and again. Why do we do what we do…because what we do is important.

It's important to our country, to our families and to each other. You don't need to look farther than Article 1 of the Code of Conduct to realize what Service means.

"I am an American fighting in the forces which guard my country and our way of life. I am prepared to give my life in their defense." …… prepared to give my life.

*As we look at what tomorrow brings…going down a fastrope, keeping those old birds flying, or the War on Terrorism, remember we're a team of teams in Service of our country…and that's what the Air Force means…..
Thank You.*

THE ALPHA MALE

Everyone has heard of the Alpha Male (AM) before…
it's the lead dog in a pack. At home the Alpha Male is
usually the Dad. Even over your own pet dog the man
of the house is the AM.

In the military we also have the AM or, the "*Ken Howk
of Silver Team*" as Tracy Barnett would say. The AM
was either the ranking dude or the baddest dude and
no one could mess with him or if he tried, the AM
would pounce on him.

You know you're not the AM if you can't squash
someone after he crossed the line. The AM adds order;
he ensures there is a hierarchy; a chain of command
if you will. In my perception, I've been the AM
"informally" and am the AM "formally."

Now men will be men and try to exert some influence
to become the AM. Some times you have to let that
happen as your men mature. Let them try to take a
shot at the title if you will. Wolves don't become the
AM without first getting their butt kicked a few times
in their lives. It's all part of growing up.

Being the AM brings with it certain responsibilities.
As the AM you need to clean up the crap so to speak.

If the formal chain isn't working the AM needs to make it happen. Remember in *Escape from Alcatraz*, the old black guy that sat up on the top step in prison that Eastwood went to rap with. He was the AM. He got there from his experience, he exerted his influence when needed, and he cleaned up the crap when he had to.

Now some guys (non AM) would not like that you actually existed. One, because they probably grew up with a domineering father (like me) and have never been able to become one. And two, probably will never become the AM and are upset that you are. And so hated you because you were and they couldn't do anything about it.

The AM is meant to be a good thing for a military unit. It's not all bad; it's mostly good. Military units need to know who the AM is. Your commander could get his AM to take care of the scut work. If your commander didn't have you do the scut work, clean up the mess, or bust some heads... you weren't the AM or he couldn't count on you.

Perception is Reality

This phrase is pretty insightful. If "I" believe something is true, it's because I perceive it to be true, so it's the truth, to me. Conversely if you perceive something to be true, then it is true to you or your reality. Your perception is your reality. Remember what I said about getting your education? As you become more educated your perspective becomes better.

Humans perceive things in their environment differently, consequently they form judgments based on their perceptions. Their perceptions are developed from their intelligence, experience, upbringing, values and everything else you are exposed to in your life.

Now hopefully as you become smarter and/or more experienced your perception is actually reality and not your version of reality.

Just because it's your perception, doesn't mean you are actually right. It just means you think you're right. Why is knowing this important? Because it helps you understand where your people are coming from and conversely your people should realize where you're coming from. If you understand their perception, you'll understand why they think the way they do, or do what they do. Here is a stance I take when I <u>know</u> I am

116

right…whether you agree with me or not is irrelevant if I <u>know</u> I'm right. Some people hate it when people disagree with them. That means you go through life hating a lot and hate is bad.

A problem with someone sticking to perception is reality is they may believe there is nothing that can change their mind, even logical explanations. So you would have to convince them that their perception wasn't reality but yours was. Kind of like when Beranger said in *Platoon*, "*You guys smoking that (*stuff*) to escape reality? I am reality.*"

I'll entertain you for a while or try to teach you why your perception is skewed, but at the end of the day, when you ain't getting it, I'd exert my will and you'd do it my way. Who cares if you still don't agree with me? Walk a mile in my shoes and you'll realize where I'm coming from.

So your perceptions are developed from your life's experiences; everyone's are different based on everyone being different. So if you understand everyone perceives things differently, you become a better leader since you'll see things from a different perspective and at the same time understand why your troops act a certain way to a certain issue.

Yelling, Chewing Butt, Etc.

One of the tools in a SNCO's toolbox is "ripping backsides." Meaning every once in a while you need to yell, or "get some" to make a point or correct behavior. I've been around some amazing "butt chewers," pardon the pun. Some that could even make a preacher cry I'm sure.

The point of this section is to not celebrate that I had a knack for yelling but to show that this is a method, a tool if you will, if used correctly. It has a positive effect if used appropriately and conversely a negative effect if used inappropriately. Also realize that some people don't respond well to yelling. So you must find another technique. That's all it is…a technique.

I grew up getting yelled and have been yelled at most of my life, I'm pretty much over being upset at actually being yelled at. Normally, if I got yelled at, it was probably for a good reason. Yelling is pretty much a part of intimidation. If you could be intimidated then it worked on you or the guy you were using it on. If a guy couldn't be intimidated or was an inappropriate technique then it didn't work.

Eventually, if all you have is a hammer then all your problems look like nails. I can't count how many times the butt chewing I used or someone used in the past didn't work. However, if used judiciously and at the right time, there aren't many better techniques.

Some rules apply to taking a chunk of butt. You probably need to be right. Some would say the Alpha Male doesn't need to be right, he just needs to be the Alpha Male and that makes him right. But more often than not, if you're right, then your reason may be justifiable.

You have to at least have some level of respect in your organization. If you don't have any or little, you can chew butt all day and even your dog won't listen. It means more when the yeller has a certain amount of juice or power in the unit.

You have to be able to instill a little bit of fear or intimidation. If not, it's wasted energy. If people don't cringe or go, "holy crap," then you can't use this technique. To get people to go, "holy crap," takes a few factors. You are actually a scary dude. You actually make people cry. You are loved so much that people can't believe they screwed up so bad as to warrant a butt reaming from you. Or the people you yell at are actually wimps. And a few other factors.

The best leaders, supervisors, and managers use all the tools they have available. To master all, you must have them in your toolbox and be trained and capable of using them. A key point to remember in all this is use the correct technique. If yelling needs to be used, let it fly. Every once in a while you need to say "get your crap together!!" in public.

Don't overuse this or any technique. Know your people. Know what techniques work with them. Don't play games but know how to motivate for action.

THE UNIT COMMANDER

How a unit is, how it acts, how it appears, how well it does its missions, the professionalism, discipline and motivation of its people, how its viewed by others... everything; can be attributed to its leadership. The unit is and forever will be judged by its leadership first.

In some units, there may be poor leadership but the people hacking the mission are so squared away, they propel the unit anyway. Although these instances are rare. A unit's leadership obviously starts with the commander.

I've been lucky to have worked with some great commanders. I've also worked with some not so good. Great commanders obviously make a unit better. All have different ways of doing some things but all have some common denominators. If you emulate these common denominators you'll become a more successful leader at any level in an organization.

Commanders are normally in a unit for a short period of time, relatively speaking. So they must hit the ground running. The commander must get his key leaders on his page, give the unit a vision and goals, and lead by example in word and deed...out front. They must exemplify the AF Core Values and must exceed the standards of Character, Competence, and Commitment.

Major Eric Ray (at the time of this book's first writing) is my commander at the 321 STS. He has a terrific leadership style and immediately garnered respect when he arrived. His reputation preceded him. Reputations always do. We knew he had done well in all his previous jobs (Flight Commander, Director of Operations, and acting Commander). We also knew he went to war and excelled. Maj Ray is an extremely intelligent, insightful, consistent, and respected commander.

Maj Ray was one of my students when I was at the Combat Control School. I rode him hard as I do with most students especially the senior ones. I did it mainly because they would be leading our Special Tactics troops in the near future and CCS wasn't a place to cruise for them. But also I wanted to get the most out of every student. He never once lost his cool, despite often conflicting and impossible tasks imposed by the cadre. His leadership style was well received by his class since we never saw conflicts in public at the team level. At that point I knew Maj Ray had a lot of character.

I'm lucky to have Maj Ray as a commander and supervisor. He has given me so much responsibility and authority...huge motivators to a guy like me. After 18 years in the military I'm well aware of the right things to do with a supervisor and a commander. Bottom line: keep the boss informed. Make things happen. Give him constructive feedback. Accept and apply his constructive feedback. Support the boss. Lead by example...from the front. I do all these and in return he gives me an immense amount of support and trust.

Maj Ray is a great man to work for. He is a great listener. He tells me like it is. He allows me to be me. As most who know me know, I'm a different sort of animal. I'm in your face, energetic, committed, not often humble, loud, opinionated, and above all else loyal. Maj Ray knows this and lets me be myself. Like I said he has given me a huge amount of responsibility, authority, trust, and support. For that, I'm forever appreciative.

But not only is his leadership a positive thing for me, more importantly, it's a positive thing for our unit. He is very likable by the troops. He is very respected by the troops. He leads by example in everything. He is the first to brag about his outstanding people. He's a huge supporter of people and families. He has a sense of humor and uses it.

One thing he instituted when he arrived was mandatory team PT. By his own admission, it is the one time a week he gets to spend with the whole squadron. Sure there were grumblings initially, but morale has never been higher. People who weren't big PTers have shown remarkable improvement and feel better about themselves. He leads it each and every week, by example...from the front. Sure there is subtle competition but it's healthy. In just this one simple thing his decisiveness, consistency, and example have made us a better unit.

Along with his character, Maj Ray is extremely competent. He understands how the ground and air integrate in war. He can easily articulate our unit's capabilities and strengths and where we're best utilized. He understands the synergy of a team composition for any mission. Maj Ray can also articulate the bigger picture command lines and how it "should" work and how to make it work when it's designed unclearly.

Maj Ray is also savvy with computer technology, which is critical these days. He is one of a few that uses technology and it actually makes him more efficient. Unlike me, I'm still on the merge lane of the information superhighway. In the AOC (operations center) during OIF, other squadron commanders would turn to him because he had his hands on the best available information. He had access to virtually every one of his people whether on data, voice, or sticky notes tied to a rock. Because of his uncanny ability to handle information, ascertain the real deal, and effortlessly be decisive, he would ensure we were doing what we were supposed to be doing and ultimately aided in winning the war.

I consider myself pretty adept at handling most issues that arise during the day. However, there are times when he'll decide on a course of action that I never even thought of. He's insightful and makes us think about issues in ways we wouldn't have otherwise thought about.

As a commander, his competence is first-rate. He is also extremely committed. His commitment to his family, his troops, his bosses, and to his mission are above reproach. He selflessly gives to all. His character and commitment were never more evident than during OIF. When faced with an impending war and the potential of putting 80+ troops in harms way he was faced with an awful dilemma where he couldn't do both. Suffice it to say, he made the right decision and led us in battle.

Technically, I have more years in the military than Maj Ray. One of my rules is always be learning. Around Maj Ray, I am always learning. He has made me a better

SNCO. His style with the squadron and ultimately me may at times seem subtle, but trust me, his decisive leadership, steady hand, and clear vision have kept us on a constant wave of prosperity.

Not counting my rules and axioms I chose to close this book with this chapter on Maj Ray. He is a great leader to emulate. He exemplifies the qualities of a leader and man that I hold so dear and also try to exemplify. He will never lose my loyalty, as I'm sure I'll never lose his.

Rules; Axioms; and Other True Stuff

- Learn the rules of whose ever game you're playing. That way you can master their game or beat them at it, or figure out a way of breaking their rules.

- Be yourself.

- Make sure your wife knows how much you appreciate her being a great military spouse and dealing with all the mess that she does.

- You're not allowed to whine about stuff at your retirement; you had 20+ years to whine.

- Sled dogs are allowed to whine…unless it becomes counterproductive. If they stop whining, you need to worry.

- Always take a gortex jacket, flashlight, pocketknife, wool hat, lapse tape, 550 cord, and polypro wherever you go.

- Two is one and one is none. This applies to those "widgets" you always need extra of. For example you always need an extra strobe light, pair of gloves, handset, carabineer, etc.

- Get your kit in order, immediately after you're back from your last trip…you never know when you'll leave again.

- Always be learning.

- You can't complain about something unless you have a solution.

- If a guy comes to work at 0845 (regular duty started at 0900 after PT) with "bed head," you know he didn't do PT. Fix it.

- Buy the round when it's your turn or when you first arrive.

- Don't be afraid to say something nice about someone in public. You might feel embarrassed or like you're kissing up. WRONG! Trust me, most everyone else is thinking of the same thing. If someone was a good guy and it's his going away party, or whatever, say he was a good guy.

- You're not allowed to be an aircrew guy (pilots, copilots, or navigators) and carry three (visible) knives. What are you…a Grizzly Adams wanna be? It looks stupid when aircrew carry that many knives.

- You aren't allowed to impose a limit on what level of slamming you'll accept if you're a slammer. *Slamming* was when you gave each other crap as a joke or because the other person was messing up and he needed to hear it from his teammates. In our business it was "dog eat dog." Wear your body armor to work. We all used to slam on each other every day. It built character and was a way your peers would handle those issues sometimes your boss didn't know about. Some times it was ruthless. If you couldn't handle it, you either got out or got your act together. For example you can't tell me (this actually happened) you like to slam at work, but you don't accept someone slamming on you about your wife. Wrongo sport. You must realize as a professional slammer, my limits are endless. If you want to take a shot at the title you have to know I will find your "weakness" and crush you with it.

- Always have all your gear ready to go at all times.

- Invest and save your money.

- Tell your wife and kids you love them everyday before you go to work and before you go to bed at a minimum.

- If your name ends in a vowel, you're probably a cut above most.

- You should have to wear brown t-shirts only, with desert uniforms. Black t-shirts look stupid in desert uniforms.

- You should not be allowed to wear white socks in uniform…ever. White socks in uniform look stupid.

- If you're in a meeting and you were given time to talk because it was an open forum or you were asked if you had something, then you come back later and say, "I have an alibi," get your act together. Be prepared and don't waste my time.

- You aren't allowed to talk after the Commander gave closing comments in any forum even if he says "anything else." That's just a figure of speech. The ranking guy always gets the last word.

- If an officer is screwing up, correct him; it's a rule. They'll thank you for it and you'll be helping him become a better officer.

- Always have something to write on and write with. You never know when you'll have to take some notes.

- Delegation is a sign of a good leader. Delegation gives you more time to deal with what you are paid to do…make things happen. Give "count batteries detail" to a sled dog so you can worry about the bigger details.

- To be the man you have to <u>be</u> the man.

- If you bring 9 bags on a deployment, you better not have any shortfalls.

- Keep track of your tasks accomplished and things done on paper. Chief Wayne Norrad told me once that if you write a bullet at least once a week or a few every so often about your accomplishments, before you know it you have an EPR (annual appraisal report) or award package already written. I used to laugh at guys that would jump through their butt to provide their boss inputs to an EPR or package.

- If you're the only one doing something that is different than everyone else; you're probably not right.

- Spend 10 cents on a 10-cent decision. Don't spend more time than absolutely needed deciding on an issue or taking action. If you spend a dollar on a 10-cent decision you're wasting time and time is valuable.

- Rolling your sleeves up on your BDUs like the AF way is stupid. Especially if you have small arms, like most in the AF. If it's hot enough to roll your sleeves up, it's hot enough to take your shirt off. The only exceptions are the way the Marines do it or the "cool guy" way of one to two turns up on the forearm.

- Why do they call it the "maternity BDU?" Do we actually send pregnant women to battle? I don't think so.

- Always be punctual to everything. There may also be times when you must be early. Punctuality is a sign of character.

- Take what you do seriously, but don't take yourself too seriously.

- It does matter if you win or lose. If it doesn't, then why do you keep score?

- Show me someone who is "okay" when they lose and I'll show you a loser. This isn't to say you shouldn't show good sportsmanship. However, if you don't care, you're a loser.

- It isn't "fun" to just play the game; "fun" is winning.

- You shouldn't be allowed to study for WAPS (AF testing system) or for civilian education during duty hours. It's wrong. These are personal endeavors and you shouldn't be given duty time to do them. Who cares if some bosses let their folks do it in other units; it shouldn't be allowed to happen on duty.

- People should complain up not down. SSgts shouldn't hear a MSgt complaining about something. It shows a lack of character to whine in front of those of lower rank.

- Support the boss.

- You can't whine about how busy you are if you only work from 0700 – 1600 and don't work overtime or on days off.

- Always look squared away in your appearance. You are a representative of your unit, career field, service, and nation.

- Ignorant people don't know they're being ignorant.

- Don't tell me "please leave a message and I'll call you right back" on your stupid answering machine when you won't call me back.

- If you tell me you're going to do something; then do it. It may seem simple when you don't follow through with simple promised actions; however each and every thing you don't do that you say you'll do is a lack of character and character matters.

- Never tell me how busy you are when there are great Americans that are facing bullets every day and working sometimes 20 – 36 hours at a pop; and normally around

18 hours a day. You sound stupid when you tell me how busy you are and you aren't getting shot at; sleep 6+ hours a night; and sleep next to your spouse every night. "Busy" is a matter of perspective obviously. By the way; maybe you should manage your time better or quit whining or both.

- To be respected you must give respect.

- You won't be respected if you look, dress, talk, and act like a thug.

- Your word is your bond…keep your word in all situations.

- Teach your children the value of budgeting, balancing a check book, saving, and investing.

- There is a difference between a Dad and a Father. A father by definition only needs to be there at conception. A Dad is there for a lifetime and everything in between. Be a good Dad to your children.

- When you see an Airman, Soldier, Marine, Sailor, or Coast Guardsman in public in their uniform…thank them.

ABOUT THE AUTHOR

Paul "Vinnie" Venturella was born in Pittsburgh, PA, May 20, 1967; to his Mom Joyce and his Dad Frank. He graduated Woodsville High School in Woodsville, NH then entered the United States Air Force in July 1985. His twin brother Frank and his sister Jill also served in the Air Force. He entered the Combat Control career field and has been assigned to units in Washington; England and North Carolina. He has traveled all over the world conducting Special Operations missions and training.

Vinnie had a very successful 21+ year career in the Air Force. He served mostly in Special Operations units and his most treasured aspect of his service was the people he served with and made life-long friendships with. He retired as a Chief Master Sergeant.

He received a Baccalaureate degree from Campbell University in May 2000 in Business Administration with a focus on Accounting; graduating Summa Cum Laude. He received a phenomenal amount of training and education while in the Air Force including all levels of Enlisted Professional Military Education.

He successfully completed the Certified Financial Planning Certification and Professional Education

Program from the College for Financial Planning in September 2005. He subsequently passed the Certified Financial Planner Board of Standards national examination in March 2006 and has only to complete experience requirements to receive the CERTIFIED FINANCIAL PLANNER™ designation.

He is active throughout his local and military communities including the Order of Sons of Italy Prosdocimi Lodge; Cape Fear Toastmasters; Cumberland County Business Council (CCBC); the CCBC Military Affairs Council; and his church Mt. Calvary Baptist Church.

Vinnie is currently in the financial services industry in North Carolina and can be reached at (910) 364-6419. He has been married to his wife Tammie since 1992 and they have one daughter, Meaghan.

Printed in the United States
94838LV00001B/35/A